STUDY GUIDE

to accompany

Teevan / Hewitt / White

Introduction to Sociology

A CANADIAN FOCUS

NINTH EDITION

Prepared by

James J. Teevan
University of Western Ontario (Emeritus)

PEARSON

Prentice
Hall

Toronto

ISBN-13: 978-0-13-175179-8
ISBN-10: 0-13-175179-4

Senior Acquisitions Editor: Laura Forbes
Development Editor: Alexandra Dyer
Executive Marketing Manager: Judith Allen
Production Editor: Richard di Santo
Production Coordinator: Avinash Chandra

4 5 6 DPC 11 10 09

CONTENTS

Preface iv

Chapter 1   What Is Sociology? 1

Chapter 2   Research Methods 7

Chapter 3   Culture 15

Chapter 4   Socialization 22

Chapter 5   Deviance 31

Chapter 6   Social Inequality 39

Chapter 7   Gender Relations... 47

Chapter 8   Race and Ethnic Relations 53

Chapter 9   Aging 60

Chapter 10   Families 66

Chapter 11   Religion 74

Chapter 12   Media 81

Chapter 13   Education 87

Chapter 14   Organizations and Work 93

Chapter 15   Social Movements 100

Chapter 16   Demography and Urbanization 108

Chapter 17   Social Change 115

PREFACE

This Study Guide is designed for use with the ninth edition of *Introduction to Sociology: A Canadian Focus*, edited by W.E. (Ted) Hewitt, Jerry White, and James J. Teevan. It provides students with study aids that complement the text.

For each chapter the following are included:
1.   *Chapter Objectives:* a brief overview
2.   *Key Terms and Definitions*
3.   *Self-Quiz:* multiple-choice questions
4.   *Fill in the Blanks:* a further set of questions to facilitate learning
5.   *Answers:* to all of the questions

TAKING MULTIPLE-CHOICE EXAMS

Multiple-choice exams can present very specific challenges. Due to the number of topics covered by their questions, multiple-choice exams generally require students to be familiar with a much broader range of material than do essay exams. Multiple-choice exams also usually require students to have a greater familiarity with specific details such as dates, names, or definitions than most essay exams, making it harder to "bluff." Moreover, at least some questions will be ambiguous to some students; even the best professors have difficulty making up questions that discriminate perfectly, so that in each case more students who have not prepared will miss a question than those who have. Worse, sometimes the bright student sees something in an item that is confusing, while the dull student misses it and gets the right answer. Finally, even a fully prepared student can make silly errors on multiple-choice exams. Here are some suggestions to help prepare for taking multiple-choice exams.

STUDY EARLY

Multiple-choice exams tend to focus on details, and most students cannot retain all of them at once. Learning a bit each day and then reviewing is a better strategy than last-minute cramming, which is associated with mental and physical fatigue, and then careless errors on the exam. Have a good night's sleep the night before and eat breakfast the day of the exam.

WHAT TO STUDY

Pay particular attention to fundamental terms and concepts that describe and explain both the important features and the processes of the subject matter. The introduction to each chapter and the summary should outline these topics. Pay special attention to ideas, events, or objects that form natural sequences or groupings, for they provide fertile ground for multiple-choice items. Most textbooks also highlight key definitions; these need not be memorized but should be generally known. Make sure you are fully familiar with the topics in the text that the instructors also covered in class. There was probably a reason for this emphasis.

PRACTISE

Practise on sample questions like those found in this book, or try to get hold of an old exam, perhaps in an exam bank. Practise with a friend and compare errors, trying to identify the sources of those errors. Each of you can then make up new questions for the other for further practice.

TAKING THE EXAM

First, and this is often very difficult, try to focus just on taking the exam. Do not increase the pressure with extra stressors like "I've got to ace this exam or I will not get into law school" or "My parents are really hoping I can improve this term." Just do your best.

Look over the whole exam to make sure it is complete, with no pages duplicated and none omitted. How many questions are there? Are some questions worth more than others? Is there a penalty for guessing? This first glance also allows you to decide on a pace so that all answers will be decided upon approximately 5 to 10 minutes before the time limit, permitting a final check for careless mistakes such as skipped questions or double answers. If a watch is allowed, bring a reliable one; if not, check the clock on the wall to avoid spending too much time on a few hard questions and as a result not even getting to easier ones.

ANSWERING MULTIPLE-CHOICE QUESTIONS

There are many strategies for improving performance on multiple-choice exams. The best way has already been covered: study early. Nothing boosts success like the confidence that arises from knowing the right answers.

At the exam, the following tips may help:

With your hand, cover up the possible responses to each question and focus on the stem or body of the question. This is not always possible, but it is meant to allow anticipating the correct response before being distracted by the options provided. Then, uncover the responses. If the anticipated response is there, good; circle it and check that none of the other responses is better.

ELIMINATION

If the predicted response is not listed, some of these tips can improve the odds of giving a correct answer. They revolve around eliminating even one wrong answer. With five responses there is a 20 percent chance of making a correct guess. But if one or two alternatives can be eliminated, that goes up to 25 percent and 33 percent, and to 50 percent if three can be safely ignored. None of these strategies is infallible.

Responses that use absolute words, such as "always" or "never" are less likely to be correct than ones that use conditional words such as "usually," "generally," or "probably."

"Funny" responses are added to reduce tension during the exam and are usually incorrect.

Choose "all of the above" if more than one of the other responses are probably correct.

"None of the above" is less often a correct response, but this tip has many exceptions; in any event, avoid being fooled by double negatives.

Very few instructors include trick questions, those intended to deceive; they are more likely to unintentionally write ambiguous or poorly constructed questions. Thus, more often than not, trick questions are actually created by students when they refuse to take such questions at face value.

Ask whether the answer under consideration completely addresses the question. If an answer is only partly true or is true only under certain narrow conditions, then it is more likely to be incorrect.

If, after a very best effort, there remain two equal alternatives, go with a gut feeling. If one of the two left is response "a," think about choosing the other, as instructors often do not want to give the answer away immediately and thus "a" is more often an incorrect response.

Take a few deep breaths after every five or so questions; this break can be surprisingly effective. Do not skip questions as doing so wastes time (finding them again, recalling your earlier thoughts) and at worst can lead to costly errors if, in haste, the corresponding blank has not been left on the actual answer sheet. If the answer just will not come after a minute, make a best guess and put a large question mark on the actual exam paper so you can return for a second try if time remains. These flagged questions should be kept to a bare minimum and never comprise more than 10 percent of all items.

THE ANSWER SHEET

Transfer all responses to the answer sheet at the same time, after all of the questions have been answered. This can save errors, such as skipping a question on the answer sheet and then having answers all off by one. It also makes it easier to ensure that you have filled in each bubble fully and that there are no stray marks on the page. Do a final check before handing in the answer sheet. There is no "part credit" on a multiple-choice exam; a bubble filled in incorrectly gets no credit.

Finally, check to make sure that your name, student number, and any other required information (such as which form of the exam is being taken) are correctly entered in the appropriate places.

TWO EXAMPLES

1. Which of the following was not offered as a tip in taking multiple-choice exams?

   a) eating a good breakfast
   b) breaking up studying into smaller time periods
   c) filling in the bubble sheet as you go along, to avoid skipping questions
   d) looking at the question stem before the provided answers
   e) going with a gut feeling

Eating a good breakfast is intuitively good advice, so "a" is the correct answer only if it was not mentioned in the text, and that would make it a bit like a trick question. The second response is like the first, common advice heard in other classes, too. The fourth response is remembered from the reading, so that is not it. That leaves "c" and "e." Response "c" seems to be the answer, with "e" a possibility, but "e" less so because gut feeling on the face of it sounds like a weak way to pass an exam. So it is "c." Congratulations, you have thought through the correct answer.

2. How is elimination important in taking multiple-choice exams?

   a) knocking off the "A" students increases your chances of scoring higher on the curve
   b) skipping questions and then coming back to them later is a good strategy; you can answer when your mind is clearer
   c) by highlighting the things that are unimportant, you can find out what not to study and thus, by default, what to study
   d) it increases chances of a correct response by removing those alternatives that you feel fairly confident cannot be right
   e) it explains why "none of the above" is often a good choice of answer and "all of the above" is a poor one

Very briefly, "a" is funny and a suggestion was made above about such answers; on top of that, it is an "a" response. Response "c" is silly, "b" and "e" exactly the opposite of suggestions made above, and so the correct answer is "d."

CHAPTER 1

What Is Sociology?

OBJECTIVES

1.   To be able to define sociology and distinguish it from other social sciences.

2.   To be familiar with the historical sources and development of the discipline.

3.   To understand the major theoretical positions used by sociologists to explain human interaction, including functionalist, conflict, symbolic-interactionist, and feminist perspectives.

4.   To be familiar with the history of Canadian sociology.

KEY TERMS AND DEFINITIONS

1. _Social facts_: social sources of behaviour used by sociologists to explain not individual behaviour, but group rates of behaviour.

2. _Learning theory_: the microsociological argument that individuals act and interact based on their past history of associations, rewards, and punishments, and based on observations of instruction by others.

3. _S.F_: the sociological model that portrays society as harmonious and based on consensus.

4. _rational choice theory_: the microsociological view that individuals act on the basis of what they expect will help them achieve their goals, and interact by playing cooperative and non-cooperative games with each other.

5. _Symbolic_: the sociological model that argues that individuals subjectively define and interpret their environments, that they are not fully constrained, and that their actions are based on reasons rather than causes.

6. _equilibrium_: as seen by functionalists, the normal state of society, one marked by interdependence of parts, harmony, and consensus.

7. _Conflict_: the sociological model that portrays society as marked by competition and/or exploitation.

8. _dysfunction_: the occasional, minor, and temporary disruptions in social life, as defined by functionalists.

SELF-QUIZ

1.   One of the major concerns of sociology is

   a)   to explain individual sources of behaviour
   b)   the difference between cultural transmission and cultural uniformity
   c)   to explain how membership in social groups affects individual behaviour
   d)   the source of deviant behaviour
   e)   to study the production and consumption of resources

2.   Social facts

   a)   are individual internal sources of behaviour
   b)   are explained by group structure or by the interrelationships between individuals in groups
   c)   may exist outside of individual consciousness
   d)   help people learn the content of a culture
   e)   b and c

3.   The suicide that men, Protestants, and older single people are more prone to is

   a)   fatalistic suicide
   b)   egoistic suicide
   c)   altruistic suicide
   d)   anomic suicide
   e)   alienated suicide

4.   Feminist approaches include each of the following, except

   a)   an examination of gender as one variable among many
   b)   looking at the informal and hidden aspects of social life
   c)   an examination of gender roles
   d)   a more interdisciplinary approach
   e)   acceptance of a variety of sociological models

5.   Scientific explanations are characterized by

   a)   intuition and faith
   b)   empirical testing and explanations of unique events
   c)   causal statements and common sense
   d)   simplicity and predictive ability
   e)   all of the above

6.   Fatalistic suicide is most likely to occur in societies in which

   a)   there are insufficient rules and regulations — anomi
   b)   the regulations concerning sexual behaviour are lax
   c)   enormous conflict exists in the content of norms, values, and roles
   d)   people feel trapped, with insufficient alternatives
   e)   b and c

7.   Which of the following statements is not part of the functionalist perspective?

    a)   large and complex societies are similar in structure to the human body
    b)   social change is generally gradual and a process that improves society
    c)   cultural universals help societies remain in equilibrium
    d)   social arrangements persist because they benefit society
    e)   society is marked by consensus

8.   Feminist sociology is least likely to borrow ideas from

    a)   symbolic interactionism
    b)   conflict sociology
    c)   functionalism
    d)   anglophone sociology
    e)   francophone sociology

9.   Scientific explanations should be simple, elegant, and *parsimonious,* which means

    a)   admirable, as with a work of art
    b)   generalizing rather than unique
    c)   empirical; they are synonyms
    d)   explaining the most with the least
    e)   more pure than applied

10.   Symbolic interactionism focuses on

    a)   a macro level of analysis
    b)   the place of art in society
    c)   cultural integration
    d)   the autonomy of individuals
    e)   conversational analysis in groups

11.   Weber, more than Durkheim, believed that sociology should include

    a)   linguistic relativism
    b)   subjective states of the individual
    c)   mechanical solidarity
    d)   a and c
    e)   b and c

12.   Marshall McLuhan is responsible for all of the following except

    a)   the medium is the message
    b)   Gutenberg galaxy
    c)   global village
    d)   *Understanding Media: The Extensions of Man*
    e)   the vertical mosaic

FILL IN THE BLANKS

1.   Durkheim believed that, to understand behaviour, one must not only look at individual factors but also at such things as the integration and the amount of regulation in society, factors he called ___institutions___.

2.   The first question of feminist sociology is always:
      _____?

3.   Sociology examines the effects of society on behaviour and therefore generally talks about _____ rates of behaviour and then differences in those rates.

4.   One result of the French and Industrial Revolutions was that simple, small, rural societies, which were based upon tradition, became more _____ and _____, conditions that fostered the growth of sociology.

5.   Auguste Comte, considered by some its founder, saw sociology as a secular religion as well as a science, with sociologists as _____.

6.   Harold Innis wrote how _____ (such as fur, fish, timber, iron ore, and wheat), their physical properties, how they are processed, and their location relative to transportation and markets shape political and social organization.

7.   The functionalist perspective adapted three major ideas from biology: _____, _____, and _____.

8.   In contrast to functionalism, conflict theory generally sees _____, _____, and _____ as the major forces in society.

9.   Symbolic interactionism maintains that people act on the basis of their individual perceptions and not according to any _____ social reality.

10.   Rational choice and learning theories were borrowed from other social sciences, the former from _____ and the latter from _____.

11.   Both English and French sociology in Canada had a common origin with Park at the University of Chicago and the _____ approach, the study of communities.

12.   The "marginal value" theorem is a part of _____ theory.

13. Innis, along with _____, who studied religious sects and political protest, and McLuhan were important in the development of a sociology department at _____.

14. From a functionalist perspective, the 1960s' scarcity of Canadian sociologists in Canadian universities was a _____, correctable by importing American sociologists, thus returning the system to a state of _____ .

15. Francophone sociology, compared to anglophone, is today more applied and more _____ in its orientation, and as a consequence less _____.

Answers

KEY TERMS AND DEFINITIONS

1. social facts
2. learning theory
3. functionalism
4. rational choice theory
5. symbolic interactionism
6. equilibrium
7. conflict
8. dysfunction

SELF-QUIZ

1. c
2. e
3. b
4. a
5. d
6. d
7. c
8. c
9. d
10. d
11. b
12 e

FILL IN THE BLANKS

1. social facts
2. "And what about the women"
3. group
4. urbanized, heterogeneous
5. priests
6. staples
7. function, equilibrium, development
8. power, disharmony, revolution
9. Objective
10. economics, psychology
11. human ecology
12. rational choice
13. S.D. Clark, University of Toronto
14. dysfunction, equilibrium
15. macrosociological, quantitative

CHAPTER 2

Research Methods

OBJECTIVES

1. To understand why sociologists conduct research and to appreciate the distinction between qualitative and quantitative methods.

2. To understand and be able to compare the workings of two major approaches—survey research and participant observation—on theory, complexity of model, measurement, sampling, and data analysis, and to know the advantages and disadvantages of each.

3. To be aware of other specific research alternatives, such as experiments and content analysis, as well as some general approaches to methods, including Marxist and female-friendly science.

KEY TERMS AND DEFINITIONS

1. _____: a statistical demonstration that changes in one variable coincide with changes in another variable; not to be confused with cause.

2. _____: description of the actual procedures used to measure a theoretical concept, as in IQ scores being used to measure intelligence.

3. _____: the degree to which a measure actually measures what it claims to measure.

4. _____: a method that extracts themes from communications, including letters, books, and newspapers.

5. _____: records produced by contemporaries of an event.

6. _____: explanations that arise from the data and thus are based on reality rather than on deductive logic.

7. _____: Marx's concept that research should not be *pure*, conducted for the sake of knowledge, but *applied*, undertaken to improve society.

8. _____: interpretations of primary sources made by others not immediately present at an event.

9. _____: research that takes place at one point in time as opposed to _____ research, which, because it takes place over a period of time, can detect change and better demonstrate cause.

10. _____: deriving a specific statement from a set of general statements.

11. _____: a sample in which every member of the population is eligible for inclusion and individuals are selected by chance.

12. _____: the appearance that two variables are in a causal relationship, when in fact each is an effect of a common third variable.

13. _____: making connecting links between related statements for the purpose of deriving hypotheses.

14. _____: repeating a research project in an attempt to verify earlier findings.

15. _____: taking a series of random samples in units of decreasing size, such as census tracts, then streets, then houses, then residents.

16. _____: the degree to which repeated measurements of the same variable, using the same or equivalent instruments, are equal.

17. _____: variables included in a model of behaviour that are held constant to check on apparent relationships between the independent and dependent variables.

18. _____: the group of subjects in an experiment exposed to the independent variable, as opposed to the _____ group, not exposed.

19. _____: a set of interrelated statements or propositions about a subject.

20. _____: the generalizability of research results beyond the artificial laboratory experimental situation to the real world.

21. _____: characteristics, such as age or religion, that take on different values among different individuals or groups. Those that are causes are called _____ with effects called _____.

22. _____: research strategy wherein a researcher joins a group to study it and group members are aware that they are being observed.

23. _____: Weber's view of the proper goal of sociology, in contrast to Durkheim's quest for prediction.

24. _____: making a generalization from a set of specific statements.

25._____: the examination by a researcher of someone else's data.

26._____: statement of presumed relationship between two or more variables.

27._____: application of natural science research methods to social science.

28._____: applying several research methods to the same topic so that the weaknesses of one method may be offset by the strengths of others.

29._____: a selection of people that matches the sample to the population on the basis of certain characteristics.

SELF-QUIZ

1. The research process should probably be described as
    a) funnel-like and circular
    b) linear
    c) triangular
    d) expanding
    e) logarithmic

2. Which research method attempts to keep the model quite simple by using random assignment and involving only the relevant independent and dependent variables?
    a) participant observation
    b) survey research
    c) content analysis
    d) experimental design
    e) ethnomethodology

3. Positivists would most likely use _____ in deriving their hypotheses.
    a) the construction of a generalization from a set of specific statements
    b) post-hoc explanations that arise from the data
    c) deductive logic
    d) connecting links between related statements
    e) first-person explanations of behaviour

4. Validity refers to
    a) those measures of a dependent variable taken before, not after, the introduction of an independent variable
    b) the degree to which repeated measurements of the same variable with the same instruments are equal
    c) a characteristic that takes on different values among different individuals
    d) consistency in longitudinal research
    e) none of the above

5.   Which of the following statements is true?

   a)   if a measure is not reliable, it cannot be valid
   b)   if a measure is reliable, it is also valid
   c)   generalizability is more important than validity
   d)   b and c only
   e)   a and c only

6.   In examining the relationship between alcohol consumption and date rape among 19-year-old males, _____ is the independent variable.

   a)   males
   b)   gender
   c)   age
   d)   date rape
   e)   alcohol consumption

7.   If researchers want to generalize to the total population and do not have to worry about costs, what type of sample would they draw?

   a)   systematic
   b)   accidental
   c)   quota
   d)   random
   e)   quasi-experimental

8.   When examining tables, percentages allow more useful comparisons than raw numbers. The only rule to remember about percentages is that

   a)   each category of the dependent variable must add up to 100%
   b)   each category of the independent variable must add up to 100%
   c)   each category of the dependent variable must have equal cell sizes
   d)   each category of the independent variable must have equal cell sizes
   e)   b and d

9.   Qualitative methods are marked by all of the following, except
   a)   humanism
   b)   interpretation
   c)   detachment
   d)   value orientation
   e)   b and d

10.   Many participant observers refuse to derive hypotheses from theories and instead
   a)   use deductive logic
   b)   use grounded theory
   c)   use inductive logic
   d)   a and b only
   e)   b and c only

11. The issues of validity and generalizability are related and are at the heart of the debate between survey researchers and participant observers. Survey researchers argue that participant observation is inferior because

    a) of its difficulty in making generalizations
    b) of its operationalism
    c) it elicits only verbal reports of behaviour; it does not directly observe it
    d) of its correlational nature
    e) c and d only

12. Female-friendly science would probably be most opposed to

    a) accepting personal experience
    b) positivism
    c) participant observation
    d) interdisciplinary approaches
    e) a breaking down of hierarchy

13. Which of the following is true of experimental designs?

    a) cause can be shown more easily than in survey research or participant observation
    b) it is strong in both generalizability and validity
    c) studies are easily replicable
    d) a and b only
    e) a and c only

14. Which method is least likely to be replicated?

    a) the experiment
    b) participant observation
    c) survey research
    d) content analysis
    e) Random Digit Dialling

15. Content analysis is a less frequently used sociological research tool and involves extracting themes from communications. Among its major strengths is that

    a) it is inexpensive
    b) it is strong on validity
    c) it does not allow researchers to intrude upon the data
    d) causal relationships can be demonstrated easily
    e) a and c

FILL IN THE BLANKS

1.   A list of all possible individual units in a population is called a _____.

2.   In the statement "As integration varies, suicide rates vary," integration is the _____ variable and suicide rates the _____ variable.

3.   Hypothesizing that, since religious students are less deviant, they will also be less likely to seek abortions, is an example of _____ logic.

4.   A _____ approach, which sees history as a series of conflicts over existing material arrangements, is attractive to Marxists. It maintains that the seeds for transformation exist in every society, with the new society containing seeds for its own transformation.

5.   Whether crime should be measured by arrest rates, conviction rates, or victim surveys raises the issue of _____.

6.   In examining whether the colour of the package influences ice cream sales for men and women separately, gender is the _____ variable.

7.   You do not need a phone book if you draw your sample using _____, but you will have a problem with cellphones.

8.   There are only two rules of sampling; first, a sample should be _____ of the population from which it is drawn and, second, conclusions should not be _____ beyond the groups from which the sample is drawn.

9.   As a general rule, when analyzing data in tables you should avoid examining actual numbers. _____ allow more useful comparisons to be made.

10.   Qualitative data, like quantitative data, are not objective, for all that is known about the social world is a consequence of _____.

11.   In the most simple social science experiment there are two groups of subjects: the experimental group and the control group. In a study of the effectiveness of a new drug, the _____ group would get the placebo, or sugar pill.

12.   A crucial difference between survey research and experiments is that the effects of all other variables not included in experimental models are supposed to be eliminated through the _____ of subjects to groups.

13.   Perspective (rather than theory), subjectivity, and a complex picture of a small number of cases mean we are probably describing _____.

14. Noting that Bill, John, Nick, and other boys are more aggressive than Mary, Liz, Joan, and other girls, and then concluding that boys are more aggressive than girls, is an example of _____ theory.

15. In their disputes with survey researchers, participant observers, while admitting to limited generalizability due to their small samples, lay claim to greater _____ because they observe actual _____.

16. Standpoint and the biographical method are types of _____ research.

17. Comparing experiments, survey research, and participant observation, validity is potentially strongest in _____. For generalizability, _____ may be best and the other two methods weaker. Finally, concerning cause, _____ excel and survey research is weaker.

18. Are empathy and understanding more characteristic of qualitative or quantitative methods? _____.

19. Because of their interest in social change, Marxists are more likely than functionalists to pay attention to _____ in their analysis.

20. Merely being in an experiment can alter people's behaviour as they try to please the experimenter. This is called the _____.

Answers

KEY TERMS AND DEFINITIONS

1. correlation
2. operational definition
3. validity
4. content analysis
5. primary sources
6. grounded theory
7. praxis
8. secondary sources
9. cross-sectional, longitudinal
10. deductive logic
11. random sample
12. spurious relationship
13. axiomatic logic
14. replication
15. cluster sampling

16. reliability
17. control variables
18. experimental group, control
19. theory
20. external validity
21. variables, independent variables, dependent variables
22. participant observation
23. *verstehen* (understanding)
24. inductive logic
25. secondary analysis
26. hypothesis
27. positivism
28. triangulation
29. quota sample

SELF-QUIZ

1. a
2. d
3. d
4. e
5. a
6. e
7. d
8. b
9. c
10. e
11. a
12. b
13. e
14. b
15. e

FILL IN THE BLANKS

1. sampling frame
2. independent, dependent
3. deductive
4. dialectical
5. validity
6. control
7. Random Digit Dialling
8. representative, generalized
9. Percentages
10. interpretation
11. control
12. random assignment
13. participant observation
14. grounded
15. validity, behaviour
16. qualitative
17. participant observation, survey research, experiments
18. qualitative
19. history
20. Hawthorne effect

CHAPTER 3

Culture

OBJECTIVES

1.   To define culture and distinguish and understand its major sociological aspects.

2.   Generally to be aware of the existence of cultural variation and of some cultural differences between the United States and Canada.

3.   To appreciate cultural integration, the lack of cultural universals, and ethnocentrism, especially Eurocentrism, infantilization, Orientalism, and androcentrism.

4.   To understand cultural studies and how the major theories (functionalism, conflict theory, cultural materialism, and feminism) explain cultural variation.

KEY TERMS AND DEFINITIONS

1. _____ : all of the cultural elements associated with a given social group.

2. _____ : a specific set of norms and values used by a society to regulate some broad area of social life.

3. _____ : those norms that, when violated, provoke a relatively strong reaction from other group members.

4. _____ : a subset of individuals who share certain cultural elements that set them apart from others in their society.

5. _____ : people who reside in the same geographical area, communicate extensively among themselves, and share a common culture.

6. _____ : anything that (1) is shared by members of a social group; (2) is passed on to new members; and (3) affects their behaviour or perceptions of the world; it includes values, norms, and roles.

7. _____ : relatively general beliefs that define right and wrong or indicate general preferences.

8. _____ : applied to culture, the theoretical perspective that explains cultural elements by showing how they contribute to societal stability.

9. _____ : elements of culture found in all known societies.

10._____: seeing things from the perspective of one's own culture. It includes the beliefs that one's culture is superior and that what is true of one's culture is true of others.

11._____: stories of the recent past, told orally, believed to be true but actually false, reflecting unconscious fears.

12._____: relatively precise rules specifying permitted and prohibited behaviours.

13._____: form of bias in which investigators systematically associate people from other cultures with child-like traits.

14._____: those norms that, when violated, do not provoke a strong reaction on the part of other group members.

15._____: cluster of behavioural expectations associated with a particular social position within a group or society.

16._____: the interrelationship of elements in a given culture such that a change in one element can lead to changes, sometimes unexpected, in other elements.

17._____: those preferences and objects that are widely distributed across all social classes in a society.

18._____: "male-centredness," a bias that involves seeing things from a male point of view or in a way that reinforces male privilege in society.

19._____: a situation in which the behavioural expectations of one role are inconsistent with those of another concurrent role.

20._____: de-emphasizes ideas and ideology as determinants of cultures, and instead sees cultures as adaptations to the needs forced upon social groups by their specific physical environments.

21._____: bias arising from being shaped by the values and experiences of the white middle class in Western industrialized societies.

22._____: form of ethnocentrism reflecting a Western need to feel superior to Arab cultures, picturing them as exotic, strange, and feminine.

SELF-QUIZ

1.   The "McDonaldization of society" includes an emphasis on

    a)   folkways versus mores
    b)   predictability and on quantity over quality
    c)   cultural integration
    d)   urban legends
    e)   structuralism

2.   Simultaneously being a parent of a young child and a full-time worker may lead to

    a)   status enhancement
    b)   role conflict
    c)   cultural integration
    d)   anomic suicidal tendencies
    e)   egoistic suicidal tendencies

3.   Nymphomania should be coupled with

    a)   AIDS
    b)   folkways
    c)   mores
    d)   structuralism but not functionalism
    e)   satyriasis

4.   The major distinction between folkways and mores is

    a)   in the nature of the reaction to a violation of the norm and not in the content
    b)   in the content of the rule and not the nature of the reaction violation produces
    c)   in the nature of the reaction to a violation *and* in the content of the rule
    d)   in neither the reaction nor the content
    e)   this question cannot be answered without more information

5.   Which of the following most likely involves a violation of a folkway?

    a)   a childless couple
    b)   income tax evasion
    c)   having three spouses at the same time
    d)   fatalistic suicide
    e)   egoistic suicide

6.   According to a conflict interpretation, Mother Theresa can be criticized for

    a)   being too good and thus discouraging others
    b)   not helping enough in her native Yugoslavia
    c)   deflecting attention from the real issue, that is, inequality
    d)   her androcentrism
    e)   a and c

7.   Which of the following is false?

   a)   most laws are social norms
   b)   most social norms are laws
   c)   many of the norms that structure behaviour are implicit
   d)   norms include mores and folkways
   e)   b and c

8.   Barbie reinforces stereotypical female traits except with respect to

   a)   being a wife and mother
   b)   being well dressed
   c)   being heterosexual
   d)   her occupation
   e)   being a consumer

9.   Which of the following groups living in Canada could not constitute a subculture?

   a)   Jews
   b)   Italians
   c)   Iranians
   d)   Inuit
   e)   a through d are all subcultures

10.   Investigators of culture have consistently found that

   a)   cultures exhibit enormous variation in their values, norms, and roles
   b)   the elements of culture in a given society are often interrelated
   c)   only a few cultural elements are common to all known societies
   d)   a and b
   e)   a, b, and c

11.   According to Lipset, which of the following factors did not contribute to Canada's greater emphasis (in comparison to the American emphasis) on group harmony?

   a)   Canada's strong ties to the British monarchy
   b)   similar frontier experiences in the two countries
   c)   the dominant religion in English Canada being Anglican
   d)   the dominant religion in French Canada being Roman Catholic
   e)   none of the above

12.   Which of the following can be classified as an object of popular culture?

   a)   a television set
   b)   a collection of Mozart's works
   c)   a KFC franchise
   d)   an antique automobile
   e)   a and c only

13.   Lipstick messages on mirrors welcoming men to the world of AIDS illustrated

    a)   urban legends
    b)   popular culture
    c)   cultural materialism
    d)   American versus Canadian value differences
    e)   mores

14.   Which perspective would explain a norm by showing how it contributes to the survival of the society in which it is found?

    a)   cultural materialism
    b)   functionalism
    c)   conflict sociology
    d)   symbolic interactionism
    e)   feminism

15.   *Berdache* is most closely associated with

    a)   religious sacrificial rites
    b)   fishing
    c)   the Arapesh
    d)   androcentricism
    e)   being two-spirited

FILL IN THE BLANKS

1.   The elements of culture that sociologists consider the most important are
_____, _____, and _____.

2.   A ban on the eating of pork versus a ban on eating a dog was used to illustrate the difference between _____ and _____.

3.   The belief that all societies should have a leader illustrated _____.

4.   The discussion of the wet-nurse was used to show that the role of _____, as we understand it, is not universal.

5.   Use of the term "hunting and gathering societies" rather than "gathering and hunting societies" can be used to illustrate the ethnocentrism of _____.

6.   Margaret Mead (1935) discovered cultural variation in sex roles. In Mundugumor society, both males and females were expected to be _____. Among the Arapesh, both sexes were to be _____. Among the Tchambuli, _____ was associated with females and _____ with males.

7.   Most social anthropologists during the nineteenth century believed that societies pass through three stages: _____, _____, and _____. Such labels are an example of ethnocentrism.

8.   _____ represents an interdisciplinary approach to the study of culture, one that is increasingly popular among sociologists.

9.   The disintegration of the Yir Yoront culture after the introduction of steel axes is an extreme example of the importance of _____.

10.   Malinowski's explanation of the Trobrianders' use of magic in the ocean but not lagoon fishing uses the _____ perspective.

_____

Answers

KEY TERMS AND DEFINITIONS

1. culture
2. institution
3. mores
4. subculture
5. society
6. cultural element
7. values
8. functionalism

9. cultural universals
10. ethnocentrism
11. urban legends
12. norms
13. infantilization
14. folkways
15. role
16. cultural integration

17. popular culture
18. androcentrism
19. role conflict
20. cultural materialism
21. Eurocentrism
22. Orientalism

SELF-QUIZ

1. b
2. b
3. e
4. a
5. a

6. c
7. b
8. a
9. e
10. e

11. b
12. a
13. a
14. b
15. e

FILL IN THE BLANKS

1. values, norms, roles
2. mores and folkways
3. Eurocentrism
4. mother role
5. androcentrism
6. aggressive, passive, aggression, passivity
7. savagery, barbarism, civilization,
8. Cultural studies
9. cultural integration
10. functionalist

CHAPTER 4

Socialization

OBJECTIVES

1.   To use a variety of perspectives to define socialization and to introduce the nature–nurture debate.

2.   To be aware of differences in the functionalist, conflict, and symbolic interactionist perspectives on socialization.

3.   Using identity formation in the transition to adulthood, to identify various socialization agents and contexts and describe how they have changed over the past 200 years.

KEY TERMS AND DEFINITIONS

1. _____ :   the means by which one is taught to live with other humans.

2. _____ :   the ways in which current privilege and status in society are passed on to the next generation.

3. _____ :   directions for people regarding what to do, when to do it, why, where, and with whom; they help in the transition to adulthood.

4. _____ :   Cooley's idea that personality is shaped as individuals see themselves mirrored in the reactions of others.

5. _____ :   G.H. Mead's term for attempts by individuals to put themselves in others' shoes, to imagine what the others are thinking, thus enabling them to see themselves as others see them.

6. _____ :   the learning of the attitudes, beliefs, and behaviours related to the roles that individuals expect to play in the future.

7. _____ :   socialization attempts that have unintended consequences.

8. _____ :   the process by which life course paths are preference-based, placing demands on people to be self-socializing.

9. _____ :   persons whose attitudes and opinions affect one's life: family, friends, and people of prestige, such as teachers and celebrities.

10._____: the debate over the extent to which human behaviour is affected by genetic versus social factors.

11._____: that which occurs when a person is not exposed to all of the experiences necessary to function in certain roles.

12._____: term in human development theory that compares a person to a flower, with preset stages of growth, the outcome of which is determined by how well or poorly the environment nurtures it.

13._____: socialization processes that lack continuity between contexts, thus making transitions to new contexts difficult.

14._____: an individual's conception of what is expected of normative behaviour; it provides a unified basis for self-reference.

15._____: interrelated sets of social positions based on a division of labour in which people share common expectations about desired outcomes.

16._____: the two aspects of Mead's conception of the self; the first impulsive and creative, the second more deliberative and cautious.

17._____: the number of socializers versus those being socialized; the lower the figure, the less the process will change those being socialized.

18._____: process in which people construct their own life course by coming to terms with opportunities and constraints, selecting pathways, and acting and appraising the consequences of their actions.

19._____: cultures in which relations between parents and offspring are governed by traditional norms accepted by both generations. In contrast is _____, where social change weakens inter-generational linkages, and _____, where parental experiences are so dated that children disregard their guidance.

SELF-QUIZ

1.   Functions of socialization include

   a)   development of an individual's personality
   b)   developing the "I"
   c)   cultural transmission
   d)   a and c
   e)   a, b, and c

2.   Defining dating as "a rehearsal for playing marital roles" illustrates the concept of

   a)   resocialization
   b)   anticipatory socialization
   c)   fixation
   d)   modelling
   e)   vicarious punishment

3.   The term "cafeteria style," or choosing what feels good at the moment and from available options was used to describe

   a)   morality of constraints
   b)   peer group pressure
   c)   religiosity
   d)   teenzines
   e)   a and b

4.   Which was not one of the five contexts governing the transition to adulthood?

   a)   family
   b)   education
   c)   mass media
   d)   peer group
   e)   fashion

5.   In Samoa, Margaret Mead disproved the widespread view that adolescence must be stressful; however, the _____ needed to disprove any theory is very rare.

   a)   negative instance
   b)   exceptional alternative
   c)   symbolic interaction
   d)   prefigurative process
   e)   individualization

6.   An example of defective socialization is

   a)   that, as an unintended consequence, video games teach violence
   b)   when the school fails to provide sufficient job training
   c)   letting people out of mental hospitals without means for community re-entry
   d)   a failure of maternal instinct
   e)   like, being so last year

7.   A postfigurative society is more likely to use _____ parenting styles, and a prefigurative society will likely use _____ parenting.

   a)   permissive, authoritative
   b)   authoritative, permissive
   c)   informal, avuncular
   d)   feminist, permissive
   e)   reinforcing, punishing

8.   Which theory argues that individuals have a view or sense of themselves that is defined and affected by the actions and reactions of others toward them?

   a)   storm and stress
   b)   Freud's personality development theory
   c)   symbolic interactionism
   d)   modelling theory
   e)   none of the above

9.   The development of the self takes place in which of G.H. Mead's stages?

   a)   the play stage
   b)   the latency stage
   c)   the symbolic stage
   d)   the looking-glass self stage
   e)   the reality stage

10.   In the play stage children imagine how others see them, and the basis for their behaviour moves from mere _____ to more reflective self-direction.

   a)   symbolism
   b)   imitation
   c)   agency
   d)   anticipation
   e)   morality of realism

11.   The _____ socialization context has diminished in importance while the _____ context has increased over the last two centuries.

   a)   peer, media
   b)   peer, religious
   c)   family, peer
   d)   religious, family
   e)   education, peer

12.   According to Bettelheim, most feral children are probably

   a)   retarded
   b)   fetal-alcohol syndrome victims
   c)   prefigurative
   d)   postfigurative
   e)   autistic

13.   Critics of education point to a _____ that communicates tacit expectations about class, gender, and ethnicity that then reduce self-esteem and educational attainment.

a) pedagogy
b) false economy
c) hidden curriculum
d) consumerism
e) emphasis on sports

14.   A _____ view would explain why the media deliberately do not report the adverse effects of television violence on teenagers.

a) conflict
b) surrogacy
c) vicarious
d) functionalist
e) role-taking

15.   While 1980s students wanted to be financially well off, in the 1960s students wanted to

a) support civil rights
b) experiment sexually
c) move to the United States
d) maximize their nature
e) develop a meaningful philosophy of life

16.   _____ refers to the process by which a person develops a place in society, traditionally defined in terms of an adult identity based on commitments to various productive roles contributing to social integration.

a) Formal operation
b) Conflict
c) Concise operation
d) Moral autonomy
e) Identity formation

17.   Socialization includes all of the following except

a) pressuring
b) learning behaviour
c) government control of the economy
d) teaching
e) learning of attitudes

18.   Margaret Mead was interested in the idea that adolescence is inevitably a time of

    a)   cultural relativity
    b)   latency
    c)   storm and stress
    d)   ethical dualism
    e)   moral realism

19.   *Coming of Age in Samoa* was written by

    a)   Margaret Mead
    b)   Ruth Benedict
    c)   Erik Erikson
    d)   G.H. Mead
    e)   Charles Cooley

20.   Marketers have several ways to make people think that consuming their product is "cool," but their chief strategy is _____ marketing, which uses ads critical of mindless consumerism.

    a)   price point
    b)   cerebral
    c)   liberation
    d)   discount
    e)   niche

FILL IN THE BLANKS

1.   The annual youth market in the United States is estimated at almost $_____, with about one-half coming from their own discretionary income. Divide that figure by ten to find the figure for Canada.

2.   The controversial _____ movement sought to perfect the human gene pool.

3.   It was not until the decade of the _____ that Canadian women surpassed men in the percentage of those still attending school full-time.

4.   Finding that adopted children are more similar to their biological parents (from whom they have been separated) than to their adoptive parents provides evidence for a _____ contribution to personality development.

5.   Disseminated through the mass media, _____ culture (as opposed to elite culture) rose to ascendance along with, and through, peer groups.

6.   It must be stressed, however, that individualization involves _____ *from* normative constraints, not _____ *to* pursue activities independent of systemic barriers such as social class disadvantage and racial discrimination.

7.   Steinberg concluded that, regardless of background, children have better outcomes when exposed to _____ parenting.

8.   To become "good prisoners" inmates often have to replace old roles and thoughts with new ones. This is an example of _____.

9.   Disagreements about how much free will people possess in their interactions with the social structure is more broadly known as the _____ debate.

10.   The _____ (Thomas, 1923) refers to thought processes people use to interpret their environments. They may then act on these interpretations.

11.   Strictly speaking, while puberty is a biological phenomenon, _____ is cultural phenomenon.

12.   A _____ effect occurs when children give up activities such as physical exercise and reading, and instead watch television, play video games, or surf the Internet.

13.   The word _____ was coined by marketers and did not come into usage until the late 1930s.

14.   In _____, a form of peer-to-peer marketing, "cool" people are hired to encourage friends or strangers to try or to buy a product.

15.   _____ refers to the process by which a person develops a place in society, traditionally defined in terms of an adult identity based on commitments to various productive roles contributing to social integration. *[If you are paying close attention, you will notice that this was one of the multiple-choice questions. Often examiners miss the fact that they have repeated a question.]*

16.   Students who attend _____ schools get better grades, attend more often, participate in more extracurricular activities, and are less likely to be in a clique or gang.

17.   The _____ involves viewing individuals as lacking the agency to resist social pressures.

18.   Tolerance that arises from reduced ethnocentrism is called cultural _____.

19.   After a boring lecture you refrain from sharing this perception with your teacher, thus showing that G.H. Mead's _____ aspect of the self is operating.

20.   On Valentine's Day you might send a card to your _____ other.

_____

Answers

KEY TERMS AND DEFINITIONS

1. socialization
2. social reproduction
3. normative structure
4. looking-glass self
5. role-taking
6. anticipatory socialization
7. defective socialization
8. individualization
9. significant others
10. nature versus. nurture
11. inadequate socialization
12. epigenetic
13. disjunctive socialization
14. generalized other
15. role system
16. "I," "me"
17. socialization ratio
18. self-socialization
19. postfigurative, cofigurative, prefigurative

SELF-QUIZ

1. d
2. b
3. c
4. e
5. a
6. a
7. b
8. c
9. a
10. b
11. c
12. e
13. c
14. a
15. e
16. e
17. c
18. c
19. a
20. c

FILL IN THE BLANKS

1. 300 billion
2. eugenics
3. 1990s
4. genetic
5. popular
6. freedoms
7. authoritative
8. resocialization
9. structure–agency
10. definition of the situation
11. adolescence
12. displacement
13. "teenager"
14. viral marketing
15. Identity formation
16. smaller
17. oversocialized conception of humanity
18. relativity
19. me
20. significant

CHAPTER 5

Deviance

OBJECTIVES

1. To argue that deviance is remarkably common and that it varies across cultures and subcultures, and throughout history.

2. To know the strengths and weaknesses of various data sources on crime.

3. To understand the need for an audience reaction to deviance and how this affects official rates of deviance.

4. To be familiar with the various theories of deviance—each one incomplete and in need of the others.

KEY TERMS AND DEFINITIONS

1. _____ : term that describes the state of normlessness, a large-scale breakdown of rules caused by a widespread discrepancy between a society's goals and the legitimate means it provides to achieve those goals, eventually leading to deviance.

2. _____ : this view argues that the economic elite is the single major force behind definitions of what is and what is not deviant.

3. _____ : the term given to behaviour that violates a norm, which implies a value judgment that the behaviour is wrong.

4. _____ : those broad structures of feeling that have changed over time such that modern individuals are now more easily and deeply offended by things that people from other times found unremarkable. The unfortunate (because it seems to entail a value judgment about society becoming better) term used to describe this phenomenon is

_____ .

5. _____ : finding illegitimate means, one of Merton's four deviant adaptations to the problems created when society provides insufficient means to achieve its goals. The other three are: _____ , watering down goals; _____ , giving up goals and means; and _____ , seeking new goals and new means.

6. _____: term for social rules that govern interpersonal relations; they are learned through socialization and are so ingrained that most become aware of them only when they are broken; also called _____.

7. _____: theory of deviance that sees individuals interacting with people who value deviance and learning from them an excess of pro-deviant perspectives.

8. _____: the filtering process through which the actual number of crimes committed is reduced due to things such as fear of reporting, bias, human error, and official reactions.

9. _____: type of deviance that is widespread and caused by diverse factors such as anomie or differential association.

10. _____: these surveys provide a sense of the types and number of crimes that are not reported to the police.

11. _____: people who commit deviant acts, but no one responds by punishing them, either because they are not caught or, if caught, because they are excused for some reason.

12. _____: belief that people routinely behave rationally, even in criminal activities, by considering the anticipated benefits and costs of their actions.

13. _____: part of labelling theory, it points out how primary deviance is unwittingly turned into secondary deviance.

14. _____: this happens when a crime prevention strategy fails because it merely moves crime from more secure to less secure targets.

15. _____: a characteristic, behaviour, or attribute that is deeply discrediting.

16. _____: arising from a sexist view, it is the tendency to blame different forms of psychiatric illness as causing women's vs. men's problems.

17. _____: its aim is to deter crime through the rational and calibrated use of the state's formal system of punishment.

18. _____: its aim is to reduce crime, not through punishment but by making it harder for people to commit crimes, by means of things like target hardening and enhanced visibility.

19._____: sanctions undertaken by the state, including courts and prisons.

20._____: behaviour officially recognized by the state as seriously anti-social.

21._____: these come from individuals or groups and include shaming, gossip, ridicule, and occasionally even exclusion from the group.

22._____: explanation for gender differences in crime, one that looks at parents and how their children learn sex roles.

23._____: view that, with greater job opportunities, women will engage in more crime, just like their male counterparts.

24._____: orientation recognizing that what counts as deviance varies across cultures and through history, and therefore does not judge it.

25._____: shared expectations of behaviour that prescribe what is culturally appropriate or desirable. If they involve a double standard, a different one for men and women, they are called _____.

26._____: people who seek to influence the making of rules and definitions of deviance.

27._____: these ask people about the crimes they have committed (such as tax evasion, impaired driving, and theft) over the previous year, and show that crime is a common phenomenon and not undertaken just by a few notorious individuals.

28._____: view that various segments of society, and not just one dominant elite, compete to have their definitions of deviance accepted.

29._____: a way of life in opposition to, as opposed to merely distinct from, the larger culture, sometimes found among delinquent boys.

30._____: Cohen's term for the tendency of working-class delinquents to invert middle-class values as a form of protest.

31._____: rationalizations that allow deviants to reduce their guilt by defining their behaviour as acceptable.

32._____: the unknown and unmeasured volume of crime.

33._____: a method for studying crime in which researchers accompany criminals on their day-to-day routines.

SELF-QUIZ

1. In arguing that stores can afford a bit of shoplifting, a thief is using which technique of neutralization?

    a) denial of personal responsibility
    b) denial of injury
    c) condemning the condemners
    d) denial of the victim
    e) appeal to higher loyalties

2. Which does not describe crack dealers?

    a) fairly well-off after a while in the business
    b) Grade 10 education
    c) wearing flashy clothes and jewellery
    d) they do not like having a boss
    e) lacking credentials

3. The crime funnel showed that for break and enter the chance of going to prison or penitentiary is about _____ percent.

    a) 0.5
    b) 2
    c) 10
    d) 25
    e) 50

4. Strain theory was not criticized for

    a) ignoring upper-class crime
    b) ignoring women's crime
    c) being too pro-police
    d) ignoring illegitimate opportunities
    e) actually, strain theory was criticized for none of the above

5. Toilet doors that open after 20 minutes, an emergency phone, and blue lights that make it harder to find a vein are part of which part of environmental criminology?

    a) enhanced visibility
    b) target hardening
    c) more eyes on public spaces
    d) general deterrence
    e) choice

6.   Biological explanations of deviance are criticized for

a)   being atavistic
b)   often ignoring women
c)   being unable to account for fluctuations in deviance rates over time
d)   a and b
e)   b and c

7.   Arguing that you learned to shoplift because your friends taught you that such behaviour is acceptable would be consistent with _____ theory.

a)   anomie
b)   differential association
c)   labelling
d)   deviance amplification
e)   relative deprivation

8.   Since 1991 crime in Canada

a)   has gone up due to the greater number of immigrants
b)   has gone up, but for reasons other than the greater number of immigrants
c)   has fluctuated greatly allowing no general statement
d)   has been relatively constant except for sexual assaults, which are up
e)   has gone down

9.   Cloward and Ohlin criticized Merton's theory of anomie because it ignored

a)   the need for access to illegitimate means
b)   that deviance is caused by biological, psychological, *and* social factors
c)   that deviance does not exist without a reaction
d)   that calling attention to minor deviance may encourage major deviance
e)   none of the above

10.   In classical criminology, for crime to be deterred the punishment must be certain and also

a)   physical
b)   mental
c)   swift
d)   lengthy
e)   both physical and mental

11.   Crimes committed by the powerful would be hardest to explain using _____ theory.

a)   classical
b)   Foucault's
c)   environmental
d)   anomie
e)   psychological

12.   Which problem was not mentioned in arguments against collecting crime statistics by race and ethnic categories?

    a)   difficulties in measuring race and ethnicity
    b)   the need to examine age and social class factors
    c)   the fact that some types of crimes get less police attention than others
    d)   the fact that deviance needs a reaction as well as an action
    e)   neither a nor c was mentioned

13.   The functions of deviance do not include

    a)   acting as a safety valve
    b)   providing employment for criminologists
    c)   marking the bottom layer of society
    d)   warning society by acting like a smoke detector
    e)   the redistribution of wealth

14.   The most common violent crime in Canada is

    a)   abduction
    b)   robbery
    c)   break and enter
    d)   sexual assault
    e)   assault

15.   Rape in warfare has been attributed to

    a)   the social cohesion it engenders among the rapists
    b)   political reasons
    c)   how it unifies the different layers of society
    d)   a and b only
    e)   b and c only

FILL IN THE BLANKS

1.   _____ theorists are generally uninterested in reducing crime and instead want to unmask the structural differences in power that shape which things are (and are not) treated as crime.

2.   Hagan estimated that 25 percent of all Canadians suffer from _____ impairment, but only half of them see a doctor.

3.   The _____, that is, the perfect abdominal muscles, is evidence of how males are drawn into the cult of beauty.

4.   The deviance committed after a social reaction and perhaps unintentionally arising from that reaction is called _____.

5.   Freudians might see mental illness as due to the inability of the _____ to handle conflicts among the id, superego, and the external world.

6.   Crime statistics are not really a measure of crime but a measure of _____ .

7.   Foucault was suspicious of eighteenth-century prison changes that placed less emphasis on punishment and more on _____; instead he saw them as an expansion of power.

8.   Working-class people who live in modest homes, have older cars, and take few vacations are called _____ and still considered deviant in Merton's anomie scheme.

9.   In a process called _____, "deviant" becomes the master status of those so labelled, that is, it becomes the dominant way in which they are identified. Even past non-deviant behaviour may be retrospectively defined as deviant.

10.   Probably _____ percent of all rapes are acquaintance rapes, involving not a stranger but someone the victim knows.

11.   Lifts, peels, and tucks are forms of _____.

12.   Dr. David Matlock practises on animal parts, has a long waiting list, calls himself an artist, and promises a more youthful appearance as he creates _____.

13.   Cohen's delinquent boys, according to the text, are similar to Merton's _____.

14.   The need for a reaction as well as an action for deviance led to a discussion of _____ versus _____, the former being those not caught for their deviance, the latter being those who are caught.

15.   An important criticism of _____ research is that it tends, in its explanations of crime, to focus on people low on the social spectrum such as members of street gangs, homeless individuals, and street-level drug dealers.

Answers

KEY TERMS AND DEFINITIONS

1. anomie
2. critical school
3. abnormal
4. sensibilities, "civilizing process"
5. innovation, ritualism, retreatism, rebellion
6. manners, etiquette
7. differential association
8. crime funnel
9. primary deviance
10. victimization surveys
11. rule breakers
12. hedonistic calculus
13. self-fulfilling prophecy
14. displacement
15. stigma
16. pathologizing
17. classical criminology
18. environmental criminology
19. formal social control mechanisms
20. crime
21. informal social control mechanisms
22. power-control theory
23. liberation hypothesis
24. relativism
25. norms, gendered
26. moral entrepreneurs
27. self-report studies
28. pluralism
29. contraculture
30. reaction formation
31. techniques of neutralization
32. dark figure of crime
33. ethnography or participant observation

SELF-QUIZ

1.	b	5.	b	9.	a	13.	e
2.	a	6.	e	10.	c	14.	e
3.	b	7.	b	11.	d	15.	d
4.	c	8.	e	12.	b		

FILL IN THE BLANKS

1. Conflict
2. psychological
3. "sixpack"
4. primary deviance
5. ego
6. police activity
7. reform
8. ritualists
9. role engulfment
10. 90
11. cosmetic surgery
12. "designer vaginas"
13. rebels
14. rule breakers, deviants
15. ethnographic

CHAPTER 6

Social Inequality

OBJECTIVES

1. To understand the basic concepts of social stratification: status, stratum, status hierarchies and power dimensions, ascribed and achieved status, social mobility, class, and social class.

2. To understand several of the major theories of social stratification, including Marxist, Weberian, and structural-functionalist positions.

3. To be aware of Canada's stratification structure, including the eight most important factors of social differentiation and their interrelationships: wealth and property, occupation, education, race/ethnicity, region and rural–urban location, gender, age, and political power.

4. To realize some of the major consequences of stratification for people, including its effects on life chances, lifestyles, values, and beliefs.

KEY TERMS AND DEFINITIONS

1. _____ : individuals who share an economic status or market position.

2. _____ : Marx's word for the working class, the non-owners of the means of production.

3. _____ : the combination of statuses that any one individual occupies.

4. _____ : Weber's three (as opposed to Marx's one) bases of social inequality.

5. _____ : change between a parent's and child's status in the same hierarchy.

6. _____ : movement up or down a status hierarchy.

7. _____ : position in a status hierarchy attained by individual accomplishment.

8. _____ : a Marxian category for people who occupy the same economic position but are unaware of this similarity.

9._____: the tendency for diversification and complexity in the statuses and characteristics of social life.

10._____: any one of a set of rankings along which statuses are rated in terms of their power.

11._____: movement by an individual from one status to another of similar rank within the same status hierarchy.

12._____: any position occupied by an individual in a social system.

13._____: individuals of similar economic position who possess a common identity and group consciousness, and tend to act as a social unit.

14._____: the capitalist class, as defined by Marx. It did not include the owners of small property, a group he predicted would be swallowed by larger capitalists.

15._____: sometimes called domination, it becomes a regular part of everyday human existence, usually because it is established in formal laws or accepted customs.

16._____: dissimilarity in the rankings of an individual's statuses across status hierarchies.

17._____: a position in a status hierarchy that is inherited or assigned.

18._____: movement by an individual from one status to another in the same status hierarchy during a lifetime or career.

19._____: similarity in the rankings of an individual's statuses across status hierarchies.

20._____: a Marxian category for people who occupy the same economic position, are aware of this commonality, and thus may become agents for social change.

21._____: a set of statuses of similar rank in any status hierarchy.

22._____: the general pattern of inequality, or ranking, of socially differentiated characteristics.

23._____: capacity to command resources and thereby control social situations.

SELF-QUIZ

1. It has been argued that the study of social stratification is concerned mainly with "who gets what and why." In this view social stratification is

    a) independent of power
    b) a distributive process
    c) an example of capitalism in its purest form
    d) concerned with class for itself but not class in itself
    e) a study of the micro-elements in society

2. Concerning status consistency, which is true?

    a) it probably relates more to wealth than to occupation
    b) status consistency is almost never found
    c) a high status consistency tends to indicate a "closed" stratification system
    d) it relates mainly to ascribed statuses
    e) it relates mainly to achieved statuses

3. Which of the following is (are) an ascribed status?

    a) educational status
    b) ethnic origin
    c) occupational status
    d) a and c
    e) a, b, and c

4. Porter saw political parties as engaging in _____, making policies based on what will get them re-elected rather than what is best for the nation.

    a) undemocratic government
    b) brokerage politics
    c) ideology
    d) institutionalized power
    e) domination

5. Weber's concept of power in social organizational theory can best be called

    a) conflict
    b) functional
    c) pluralist
    d) symbolic rationalist
    e) positivist

6. Marx did not advocate

    a) equal liability of all to labour
    b) centralization of credit
    c) a graduated income tax
    d) the continued distinction between town and country
    e) free education

7.   For Marx, apart from obvious differences in wealth and prestige, what really underlies the division of societies into two opposing groups is

   a)   the power derived from ownership or non-ownership of property
   b)   the proletariat and the bourgeoisie
   c)   the structure and the superstructure
   d)   class for itself and class in itself
   e)   none of the above

8.   Attaching greater rewards to positions deemed either crucial or requiring rare skills than to those deemed less valuable is a part of which perspective?

   a)   structural-functionalism
   b)   symbolic interactionism
   c)   pluralism
   d)   conflict
   e)   none of the above

9.   In societies such as Canada, in which wealth and property can be inherited, there is a tendency toward reduced

   a)   horizontal mobility
   b)   status consistency
   c)   vertical social mobility
   d)   generational conflict
   e)   class structure

10.   Which of the following is true concerning Canada's income distribution?

   a)   income is more widely diffused in the population today than ever before
   b)   the distribution of wealth has not changed very much in recent decades
   c)   government programs to redistribute income from the very rich to the lower strata have generally been successful
   d)   the upper strata received relatively less income in the 1990s than in the 1950s
   e)   c and d

11.   The best single indicator of an individual's general stratum position is

   a)   income
   b)   education
   c)   ethnicity
   d)   sex
   e)   occupation

12.   Which of the following statements is true?

a)   equal opportunity exists for all Canadians to acquire education
b)   in Canada today ascriptive traits are still related to educational achievement, although perhaps less so than historically
c)   inequality of access has little to do with different education levels
d)   Canada's universal access to education has guaranteed an open stratification system
e)   a and d only

13.   According to Porter, Canada resembles a "vertical mosaic," a social structure

a)   marked by a high degree of status consistency
b)   in which wealth and property can be passed on through inheritance
c)   in which the distribution of wealth is increasingly more widely diffused among various racial and ethnic groups
d)   comprising many diverse racial and ethnic groups, ranked along a hierarchy of power and privilege
e)   in which enormous variation exists in the ranking of various norms and values

14.   The "new working class" is composed of

a)   technical computer workers
b)   low-paid, semi-skilled, white-collar workers
c)   pink-collar ghetto workers
d)   the *lumpenproletariat*
e)   contract workers

15.   Which is not a characteristic of a metropolis as opposed to a hinterland?

a)   seat of political power
b)   large-scale industry
c)   large universities
d)   source of raw materials
e)   population centre

16.   Which of the following is false?

a)   women made up over 45 percent of the labour force in 2000
b)   among full-time employees, women make only 71 percent of the average male wage
c)   women's lower pay is mostly a function of their lesser training and education
d)   the female disadvantage in pay is more evident among older cohorts
e)   a through d are false

17.   Political power is associated with other power sources to determine the distribution of wealth and other resources in this country. Those who tend to dominate are

    a)   of foreign origin and live outside Canada
    b)   male and of French origin
    c)   the economic elites who live in hinterland areas
    d)   central Canadians, of British origin, and male
    e)   central Canadians and of French origin

18.   Which of the following statements is true in reference to social stratification?

    a)   those with more to spend are more likely to place greater emphasis on home life than those from the lower strata
    b)   lower-class individuals are more susceptible to a broad spectrum of physical and mental illnesses than their more prosperous counterparts
    c)   the working class tends to place less value than its counterparts on material success and financial security
    d)   due to their big jobs, daily life in the upper strata is characterized by greater restrictions than life in the lower strata
    e)   a and b

FILL IN THE BLANKS

1.   The success of government programs in alleviating economic problems can be seen in the reduction, from more than 40 percent in 1969 to 17 percent in 1999, of families headed by _____ living below the official low-income line.

2.   Evidence indicates that the top 10 percent of the Canadian population hold over _____ of all wealth; stocks and dividends are disproportionately theirs.

3.   According to Marx, history is a series of struggles between "haves" and "have-nots," today capitalist and worker, previously _____ and _____, and before that _____ and _____.

4.   Most researchers suggest that age has an up-and-down, or _____, association with stratification.

5.   _____ mobility is the best indicator of an open stratification system.

6.   The three things that have reduced the chance of a workers' revolution in Canada are the better standard of living that all enjoy, the hope for future mobility, and _____.

7.   The greatest wealth is found in the provinces of Alberta and _____, while the least is found in the _____ provinces.

8.   Marx focused not on money but on what he called the means of _____.

9.   For socialism to triumph, the working class has to become more than just a
        _____, a category of people sharing the same economic position. In
        addition, it needs an awareness of its common position and a willingness to
        mobilize for change for it to become a genuine _____.

10.   Marx suggested that two stages follow the revolution of the proletariat: first, a
        _____ phase, a dictatorship of the proletariat with the leaders of the
        revolution heading the political apparatus of the society, or the state. In the second
        stage, _____ is achieved and the state as a political force withers away.

11.   While Marx stressed conflict, group (class) action, and the singular importance of
        economic power in understanding social stratification, the structural-functionalist
        school of thought emphasizes instead _____, _____,
        and _____ of power in modern social structures.

12.   The author agrees with Marx that control of property/wealth, particularly by large
        businesses, is the most important source of _____ in modern stratifica-
        tion systems. Following Weber, he suggests that two other socioeconomic status
        hierarchies, _____ and _____, also play key roles.

13.   The distribution of _____ is the most direct measure or indication of
        how groups or individuals rank in the overall stratification system.

14.   The biggest occupational change last century was the growth of _____
        occupations and a corresponding decline of people working in _____.

15.   University graduates earn about _____ percent more than high school graduates.

16.   The major subsystems, or _____, of society include the economy,
        polity, religion, education, and agencies of social control.

17.   Education is included among the set of socioeconomic status hierarchies, or
        power rankings, because it is closely linked to the acquisition of _____
        and _____ in modern societies.

18.   Generally the term _____ refers to the ability to lead a healthy, happy,
        and prosperous existence.

19.   Overall, the _____ ethnic group still tends to dominate the top of the
        economic power structure in Canada. The one group consistently
        underrepresented is the _____.

20.   Some say that the pervasiveness of female subordination in the stratification
        system is so great that women's position is not unlike that of a _____.

Answers

KEY TERMS AND DEFINITIONS

1. class
2. proletariat
3. status set
4. class, status group, party
5. intergenerational mobility
6. vertical mobility
7. achieved status
8. class in itself
9. social differentiation
10. status hierarchy
11. horizontal mobility
12. status
13. social class
14. bourgeoisie
15. institutionalized power
16. status inconsistency
17. ascribed status
18. intragenerational mobility
19. status consistency
20. class for itself
21. stratum
22. social stratification
23. power

SELF-QUIZ

1. b
2. c
3. b
4. b
5. c
6. d
7. a
8. a
9. c
10. b
11. e
12. b
13. d
14. b
15. d
16. c
17. d
18. b

FILL IN THE BLANKS

1. the elderly, people over 65
2. 50 percent
3. feudal lord and serf; master and slave
4. curvilinear
5. Vertical
6. worker passivity, accepting their lot
7. Ontario, Atlantic
8. production
9. class in itself, class for itself
10. socialist, communism
11. consensus, individual action, pluralism
12. power, education, occupation
13. wealth
14. white-collar, agriculture
15. 61
16. institutions
17. wealth, occupational status
18. "life chances"
19. British, Native peoples
20. visible minority group

CHAPTER 7

Gender Relations

OBJECTIVES

1. To apply the methodological skills learned in Chapter 2 to the study of gender.

2. To acknowledge social and biological antecedents of gender differences in the gendered order and the great overlap in the behaviours of women and men.

3. To appreciate the distinction between sex and gender and apply the major theoretical perspectives of the book to the study of gender.

4. To describe body norms for men and women, the gendered division of labour with respect to housework and paid work, and gendered violence.

5. To look at convergence in gender roles and its various pathways.

KEY TERMS AND DEFINITIONS

1. _____: a system of gender relations in which traits associated with men are valued more than those associated with women and which, on that basis, gives men greater privilege.

2. _____: social arrangement in which males and females, in both unpaid and paid labour, take on what are deemed "sex-appropriate" tasks.

3. _____: a variant of feminism that has one goal, the abolition of male supremacy, and two connected focuses, biological reproduction and paid labour.

4. _____: a *biological* ascribed trait that includes things like chromosomes and hormones: XX and more estrogen for a female and XY and more testosterone for a male.

5. _____: a variant of feminism that agrees that patriarchy must be eradicated, but, methodologically speaking, seeks a longer causal chain, seeing capitalism as the real issue.

6. _____: a *social* construct based on definitions of masculinity and femininity, including norms and behavioural expectations for each gender category that in turn may organize social relations.

7. _____: one's perception of self as female or male, not to be confused with sexual orientation, and not necessarily consistent with a one's sex.

8. _____: viewing someone as a thing, usually with a sexual overtone, and not fully as a person.

9. _____: site of unpaid domestic labour and what some call *expressive tasks,* nurturing and providing emotional support.

10. _____: the part of social structure that includes gendered norms, gendered roles, and a gendered ideology, which together make social life gendered, directing how males and females *should* act.

11. _____: a variant of feminism that focuses on giving greater opportunity to women and includes pay equity and employment equity policies.

12. _____: individuals possessing aspects of both genders.

13. _____: the arena of paid labour in which the *instrumental tasks* needed for survival are performed.

SELF-QUIZ

1.   The terms "masculine" and "feminine" are most closely associated with the concept of

   a)   sex
   b)   gendered order rather than gender identity
   c)   gender
   d)   ascribed status
   e)   transsexuality

2.   The position most likely to define a gendered division of labour as acceptable is

   a)   symbolic interactionism
   b)   radical feminism
   c)   socialist feminism
   d)   liberal feminism
   e)   functionalism

3.   The instrumental dimension is least likely to include

   a)   rationality
   b)   a public location
   c)   competition
   d)   emotionality
   e)   breadwinning

4.   Concerning sex-change operations, which of the following is false?

   a)   there are more male-to-female than female-to-male operations
   b)   they allow the matching of sex to gender
   c)   most operations are done on transvestites
   d)   some men may seek the operation to avoid the stigma of homosexuality
   e)   an artificial penis can be constructed

5.   To the extent he took any position, Marx's view is most similar to that of
      _____ on the gendered division of labour.

   a)   functionalists
   b)   symbolic interactionists
   c)   radical feminists
   d)   liberal feminists
   e)   the nurture side

6.   A focus on day care and pay equity would characterize _____ feminism.

   a)   maternal
   b)   liberal
   c)   socialist
   d)   radical
   e)   a and b

7.   In a binary system most individuals can be classified as either male or female.
      The other binary distinction most applicable would be

   a)   bisexual and homosexual
   b)   tomboy and sissy
   c)   XX and XY
   d)   androgynous and undifferentiated
   e)   lesbian and gay

8.   Private is to nurturing as

   a)   transsexual is to transvestite
   b)   feminine is to masculine
   c)   housework is to wifework
   d)   public is to tasks necessary for survival
   e)   private is to government

9.   Single women make about ____ cents for every dollar men make.

   a)   11
   b)   69
   c)   73
   d)   93
   e)   99, if they have good math skills

10.   Women are in the majority for all of the following employee categories except
    a)   lawyers
    b)   librarians
    c)   a and b
    d)   elementary school teachers
    e)   physiotherapists

11.   A female disadvantage of ___ cents on the dollar is probably due to discrimination.

    a)   31
    b)   27
    c)   that figure is hard to gauge, as most women get married
    d)   11
    e)   7

12.   In health matters, women do better than men in all of the following, except

    a)   declining smoking rates
    b)   homicide victims
    c)   suicide
    d)   obesity
    e)   longevity

13.   Of the following, the most general term, the one that could include the rest, is

    a)   gender norms
    b)   gender ideology
    c)   gendered order
    d)   gender inclusive language
    e)   motherwork

14.   The words "penis" and "vagina" indicate that we are talking about

    a)   transsexuality
    b)   sex
    c)   masculine and feminine
    d)   gender identity
    e)   androgyny

15.   Seeking transsexual surgery would probably be best explained using

    a)   maternal feminism
    b)   Marxist conflict theory
    c)   functionalism
    d)   symbolic interactionism
    e)   a and b

FILL IN THE BLANKS

1. The _____ is socially reproduced through the process of gender socialization.

2. It can be argued that sex is an _____ characteristic while gender is an _____ characteristic.

3. A major criticism of the functionalist view is that it justifies _____.

4. Work for pay is an _____ task; nurturing is an _____ task.

5. The science in which women's participation is closest to men's is _____.

6. Transsexuals have a discrepancy between their gender identity and their biological sex. This is much more than _____, or wearing clothes of the other sex.

7. Males are less likely than females to go to their doctor to report bulimia; they are also less likely than female victims to report a _____.

8. _____ feminism's focus is finding alternative reproductive strategies.

9. Women's work can be divided into three categories: _____, _____, and _____.

10. The term for Devor's masculine-appearing women is _____.

11. Gender identity is probably fixed by about age _____.

12. Bulimia and anorexia nervosa are manifestations of the cult of _____, in which women's self-worth is particularly defined through their appearance.

13. Role conflict was suggested as an alternative description for _____ in the workplace.

14. Violence in the home between _____ is perhaps difficult to explain as being due to patriarchy.

15. A poor self-concept for a girl can lead to _____ and then obesity. For a boy, the poor self-concept leads to _____ and then obesity.

Answers

KEY TERMS AND DEFINITIONS

1. patriarchy
2. gendered division of labour
3. radical feminism
4. sex
5. socialist feminism
6. gender
7. gender identity

8. objectification
9. private realm
10. gendered order
11. liberal feminism
12. transgendered
13. public realm

SELF-QUIZ

1. c
2. e
3. d
4. c
5. a

6. b
7. c
8. d
9. d
10. a

11. d
12. a
13. c
14. b
15. d

FILL IN THE BLANKS

1. gendered order
2. ascribed, achieved
3. an ideology of gender inequality
4. instrumental, expressive
5. biology
6. transvestitism
7. sexual assault
8. Radical

9. wifework, motherwork, housework
10. gender blenders
11. three
12. thinness
13. objectification
14. gay spouses
15. depression, physical inactivity

CHAPTER 8

Race and Ethnic Relations

OBJECTIVES

1. To understand how an immigrant community is formed.

2. To understand what is meant by ethnic, racial, and minority groups, especially in relation to the changing Canadian ethnic mosaic, and to become acquainted with such issues as prejudice, discrimination, and racist ideology.

3. To become more fully aware of the history and pattern of First Nations/European colonizer and French/English relationships.

4. To understand three interpretations of ethnic group relations—assimilationism, pluralism, and a postmodern approach—and to consider some of the implications of each for social policy.

KEY TERMS AND DEFINITIONS

1. _____ : the view that ethnic diversity gradually and inevitably declines as group members are absorbed into the general population, in the process becoming more and more like the dominant group.

2. _____ : the development of a full set of institutions in an ethnic community that parallel those in the larger society.

3. _____ : an arbitrary social category based upon inherited physical characteristics that have been defined as socially meaningful, such as skin colour or facial features.

4. _____ : mental images that exaggerate traits believed to be typical of members of a social group.

5. _____ : discrimination against members of a group that occurs as a by-product of the ordinary functioning of bureaucratic institutions, rather than as a consequence of a deliberate policy to discriminate.

6. _____ : a system of coexisting racial and ethnic groups, each of which maintains to some degree its own distinctive culture, networks, and institutions, while participating with other racial and ethnic groups in common cultural, economic, and political institutions.

7. _____ : the learning of the language, values, and customs of a dominant group by an ethnic group.

8. _____ : the hierarchical ranking of ethnic populations in a society.

9. _____: the denial of opportunities, generally available to all members of society, to some because of their membership in a social category.

10. _____: maintenance of physical distance between ethnic or racial groups.

11. _____: individuals who share a particular trait defined as socially meaningful, but who may not interact or have anything else in common.

12. _____: the domination by a settler society of an indigenous population. In time, the native population suffers the erosion of its traditional culture and usually occupies a subordinate status in the pluralist society of which it has involuntarily become a part.

13. _____: a people, a collectivity of persons who share an ascribed status based upon culture, religion, national origin, or a shared historical experience arising from a common ethnicity or race.

14. _____: prejudging people based upon characteristics they are assumed to share as members of a social category.

15. _____: approach to the study of racism that includes history, power, change, and how ideas are constructed and controlled.

16. _____: sequential movement of persons from a common place of origin to a common destination, with the assistance of relatives or acquaintances already settled in the new location.

17. _____: view, associated with multiculturalism, that ethnic diversity, stratification, and conflict remain central features in modern societies, with race and ethnicity of continuing importance in individual identity and behaviour.

18. _____: the collective designation given by assimilationists to four stages in the relationship between dominant and minority groups: contact, competition, accommodation, and finally, assimilation.

19. _____: a social category, usually ethnically or racially labelled, that occupies a subordinate rank in the social hierarchy.

20. _____: acceptance of a minority group by a dominant group into its intimate and primary social relationships.

21. _____: they regard racial or ethnic categories as natural genetic groupings and attribute behavioural and psychological differences to the genetic nature of these groupings.

22._____ : a broad strategy to increase the representation of disadvantaged groups (Aboriginal peoples, visible minorities, women, and people with disabilities) at all levels of the occupational structure.

23._____ : assigning people to socially constructed racial categories and behaving toward them as though these categories are real.

SELF-QUIZ

1. Immigrants with legal guarantees of support from relatives or others in Canada are

    a) independent
    b) examples of chain migration
    c) sponsored
    d) marginal
    e) *de jure*

2. One large factor in the development of a strong sense of solidarity, ethnic identity, and a wide range of institutions is

    a) cultural universals combined with minority-group status
    b) the size of the ethnic population
    c) whether the individuals share similar values and beliefs
    d) the difference between achieved and ascribed status
    e) the experience of three solitudes

3. Weber and Barth both suggested that ethnicity has four major dimensions. Which of the following fits into their theoretical perspective?

    a) an achieved status
    b) a subculture
    c) an ascribed status
    d) a and b
    e) b and c

4. An important feature of an ethnic group as a form of social organization is that it

    a) has acculturated
    b) is fully isolated from the mainstream of society
    c) has boundaries
    d) lacks institutional completeness
    e) has assimilated into the mainstream of society

5. A 1990 survey by Decima found that _____ percent of Canadians agreed that "all races are created equal."

    a) 90
    b) 70
    c) 50
    d) 30
    e) 10

6.   The idea of a melting pot goes best with which theoretical perspective?

    a)   colonialism
    b)   imperialism
    c)   pluralism
    d)   assimilationism
    e)   the passing on of genetic characteristics to one's ethnic group

7.   The unemployment rate for First Nations people living off-reserve is roughly _____ the rate for the rest of Canada.

    a)   equal to
    b)   double
    c)   triple
    d)   ten times
    e)   one-half

8.   Employment equity targets include all of the following except

    a)   women
    b)   the disabled
    c)   Blacks in Nova Scotia
    d)   French Canadians
    e)   First Nations

9.   Dominant groups frequently control and restrict the economic, social, and political participation of minorities by means of

    a)   expulsion
    b)   annihilation
    c)   discrimination
    d)   exploitation
    e)   disruption

10.   Which of the following statements is true?

    a)   *de jure* discrimination is more frequent than *de facto* discrimination
    b)   discriminatory behaviour is caused by prejudiced attitudes
    c)   victims of prejudice usually bring it on themselves
    d)   a prejudiced person may not discriminate and a person may discriminate yet not be prejudiced
    e)   a and b only

11.   Under the terms of the Indian Act, special status is conferred upon

    a)   the Métis
    b)   British Columbia and Manitoba Indians only
    c)   the Inuit
    d)   registered Indians
    e)   a and c only

12. The erosion of French language and culture in Canada has many sources; a main one is

   a) the recent increase in Quebec's death rate
   b) the fact that English-speaking immigrants to Canada far outnumber French-speaking immigrants
   c) the 1977 language legislation, which specified that the language of Quebec's French majority shall be the official language of Quebec
   d) the victory of the federal Progressive Conservatives in the 1980s
   e) the creation of the European Economic Community

13. Post-World War II immigration in Canada is marked by its

   a) ethnic networks
   b) institutional completeness
   c) ethnic diversity
   d) tendency toward cultural assimilation
   e) tendency toward structural assimilation

14. The postmodern theoretical approach to ethnic relations is closest to

   a) feminist thought
   b) post-feminist thought
   c) post-colonial thought
   d) structuralism
   e) functionalism

15. Endogamy is probably most important for which group below?

   a) Jews
   b) Italians
   c) Germans
   d) Ukrainians
   e) it is equally important to all groups listed

FILL IN THE BLANKS

1. It is _____, more than any other racial or ethnic group, who are likely to experience discrimination, according to a Toronto telephone poll study.

2. *Nunavut* means _____ in Inuktitut.

3. Many observers predict not a bilingual Canada but a future of _____ solitudes.

4. Comparing Winnipeg and Saskatoon to Toronto, there are relatively fewer immigrants and relatively more Aboriginals in _____.

5.   Pluralist societies, where people of various cultural, religious, or racial origins live side by side within a single social, economic, and political system, exist because of historical processes of _____, conquest, and _____.

6.   A social attribute such as ethnicity, acquired from one's parents and other ancestors and conferred at birth, is referred to as an _____.

7.   Almost one in five Canadians, including many Italians and Chinese, have a _____ other than the two official languages.

8.   The critical factor in the maintenance of ethnic group boundaries is _____, that is, marriage within one's own ethnic group.

9.   The Charter of the French Language is better known as _____.

10.   After the British and French, the largest group in Canada is the _____.

11.   In a Toronto study Italians and _____ felt well treated while Blacks and _____ felt badly treated.

12.   The _____ are those people descended from marriages between Indian women and early European settlers.

13.   A feeling or sense of group belonging with others is part of the _____ dimension of ethnicity.

14.   By setting a universalistic rule that all guards must weigh at least 70 kilograms, a security firm may effectively be practising _____.

15.   Exaggerated mental images of groups are called _____, while the attitudes associated with those images are called _____, and the behaviour sometimes associated with them _____.

16.   The _____ (1763) transferred virtually all Canadian lands under French control to the British.

17.   Ethnic residential enclaves are most characteristic of immigrants from _____.

18.   The continent now supplying most of Canada's immigrants is _____.

19.   The era of the _____ immigrant was a brief one in Canada, for the predominant pattern of immigrant settlement has always been urban.

20.   The perspective that sees the maintaining of one's immigrant ethnic culture and language as hindering upward mobility is called _____.

Answers

KEY TERMS AND DEFINITIONS

1. assimilationism
2. institutional completeness
3. race
4. stereotypes
5. systemic or institutionalized discrimination
6. pluralistic society
7. acculturation
8. vertical mosaic
9. discrimination
10. segregation
11. social category
12. colonialism
13. ethnic group
14. prejudice
15. postmodern perspective
16. chain migration
17. pluralism
18. race relations cycle
19. minority group
20. structural assimilation
21. racist ideologies
22. employment equity
23. racialization

SELF-QUIZ

1. c
2. b
3. e
4. c
5. a
6. d
7. c
8. d
9. c
10. d
11. d
12. b
13. c
14. c
15. a

FILL IN THE BLANKS

1. Blacks
2. our land
3. two unilingual
4. Winnipeg and Saskatoon
5. colonialism, migration
6. ascribed status
7. mother tongue
8. endogamy
9. Bill 101
10. Germans
11. Portuguese, South Asians
12. Métis
13. focus of identity
14. institutionalized discrimination
15. stereotypes, prejudice, discrimination
16. Treaty of Paris
17. China
18. Asia
19. farmer
20. assimilationism

CHAPTER 9

Aging

OBJECTIVES

1. To present a balanced portrait of old age and aging, including its ups and downs.

2. To learn the various theoretical approaches to aging, including activity theory, disengagement theory, exchange theory, and others.

3. To understand the importance and sources of family ties and social support in later life.

4. To be aware of the health and retirement issues facing older Canadians and the corresponding policy implications.

KEY TERMS AND DEFINITIONS

1. _____: changes that are a direct function of aging; also called *maturation*.

2. _____: an interdisciplinary study of aging that involves the physical, psychological, and social processes related to growing old and being an older person.

3. _____: outcomes that result from having been a certain age at a certain point in time and thus capture the impact of an historical era.

4. _____: a framework, with several linking concepts, compatible with a number of theoretical approaches. It involves a series of age-related transitions that occur along a trajectory across the age structure.

5. _____: the study of the physiological aspects of aging and the unique health concerns of older persons.

6. _____: macro-level view of how certain processes create a structure that tends to place restraints on the lives of older people.

7. _____: view that the withdrawal of older persons from active social life (paid work particularly) is functional for both them and society.

8. _____: approach that emphasizes subjective experiences of older people and their ability to exercise agency in negotiating with others.

9. _____ : a system of expectations and rewards based on age.

10. _____ : examines power, social action, and social meanings as part of a critique of knowledge, culture, and the economy. It includes the social construction of old age, dependency, and old-age policy.

11. _____ : a view that the best prescription for a successful old age is to take on new activities to replace those left behind.

12. _____ : a macro-level approach focused primarily on two key concepts: a structure that favours young and middle-aged adults, and an age cohort, individuals of a similar age.

13. _____ : a more conflict-oriented perspective that focuses on the weaker bargaining position of older persons caused by their lack of resources.

SELF-QUIZ

1.   By 2041, the percentage of Canadians over the age of 65 will be

   a)   3%
   b)   10%
   c)   23%
   d)   33%
   e)   50%

2.   The term *praxis* is most closely associated with _____ theory.

   a)   critical
   b)   life course
   c)   age-graded
   d)   disengagement
   e)   activity

3.   For women over the age of 75, the most common experience is

   a)   divorce
   b)   remarriage
   c)   improved health
   d)   moving in with a sibling
   e)   widowhood

4.   The _____ approach focuses on the intimate ties between generations.
    a)   social problems
    b)   critical
    c)   activity
    d)   ambivalent
    e)   solidarity perspective

5.   Institutionalization in old age is more common among women, the never married, and the

    a)   poor
    b)   childless
    c)   wealthy who can afford it
    d)   divorced
    e)   later born

6.   About ____ percent of persons aged 65 and over have at least one living sibling.
    a)   10
    b)   33
    c)   50
    d)   80
    e)   99

7.   Flexible age of retirement is associated with proponents of _____ justice and mandatory retirement with proponents of _____ justice.
    a)   individual, comparative
    b)   comparative, individual
    c)   civil, tort
    d)   feminist, patriarchal
    e)   common law, civil

8.   The average age of retirement in Canada is not 65 but closer to
    a)   70
    b)   68
    c)   62
    d)   57
    e)   55

9.   One-half of Canadians aged 65 years can expect to live another ____ years.
    a)   25
    b)   2
    c)   5
    d)   35
    e)   18

10.   And ___ of these years should be disability-free.

    a)   one-half
    b)   one-third
    c)   most
    d)   a few
    e)   4.5

FILL IN THE BLANKS

1.   _____ analysis is concerned with individual experiences of aging rather than structural influences.

2.   Everyone born in the computer age would experience similar _____ effects, but not similar age effects.

3.   Activity theory challenges _____ theory, which involves people shedding roles as they age.

4.   The two basic objectives of our retirement income system are the anti-poverty objective and, the harder to achieve _____ objective.

5.   The failure of society to adjust quickly to the lengthening of post-retirement life is an example of a _____.

6.   Some suggest that marital happiness follows a _____ pattern, with happiness greatest in the early and later years.

7.   Research on physical activity reveals that one-half of the physical decline associated with age is due not to aging per se but to _____.

8.   While most people arriving at hospital need short-term treatment for an acute problem, older people require a focus on _____ rather than cure.

9.   Over a lifetime, a _____ can mean much more in real dollars and in old-age security than a higher salary while in the labour force.

10.   Personal responsibility for aging issues would flow from Mills' concept of _____ rather than public issues.

11.   Women retirees compared to men face more inadequate _____, while the men are challenged by a lack of _____.

12.   The _____ is for pensioners with limited incomes; qualifying to receive it is used in some studies as a measure of poverty.

Answers

KEY TERMS AND DEFINITIONS

1. age effects
2. gerontology
3. period effects
4. life course perspective
5. geriatrics
6. political economy of aging perspective
7. disengagement theory
8. social constructionist perspective
9. age-graded
10. critical theory
11. activity theory
12. age-stratification perspective
13. exchange theory

SELF-QUIZ

1. c
2. a
3. e
4. e
5. b
6. d
7. a
8. c
9. e
10. a

FILL IN THE BLANKS

1. Micro-level
2. period
3. disengagement
4. earnings-replacement
5. structural lag
6. curvilinear
7. disuse
8. care
9. pension
10. private troubles
11. financial security, social contacts
12. GIS, Guaranteed Income Supplement

PAUSE

How are you doing so far? Is there a pattern in your errors, for example, knowing definitions but not specific facts, especially those involving numbers, or doing well on fill-in-the-blank but not multiple-choice questions? Are you reading too much into the multiple-choice options? They are not meant to trick you but to reinforce what you have read in the text.

Then, what can you do to help yourself? Reread the things you underlined in the text once more? Make an outline of each chapter? Do these exercises with a friend and then discuss your performance? Go to see your instructor or teaching assistant?

Problem	Suggested Solution
1.	1.
2.	2.
3.	3.

NOTES

CHAPTER 10

Families

OBJECTIVES

1. To learn terms such as "consanguine family," "exogamy," "polygamy," "matriarchy," and "patrilocality," to name a few, which reflect the variety of kinship and family forms.

2. To be exposed to differences in family patterns across societies.

3. To know both macro and micro changes in family functions.

4. To understand the life cycle of the family, from socialization for marriage, to childbearing and childrearing.

5. To appreciate the continuity in family form, despite increasing divorce and other changes.

KEY TERMS AND DEFINITIONS

1. _____ : a wife's lesser power in a marriage that may arise from her being younger than her husband.

2. _____ : the emotional dimension of marriage, including sexual gratification, companionship, and empathy.

3. _____ : marriage of persons with similar physical, psychological, or social characteristics. This is the tendency for like to marry like.

4. _____ : ongoing instrumental and expressive exchanges and a commitment that can include legal and social pressures against dissolution.

5. _____ : a nuclear family consisting of partners who are not formally married, with or without children.

6. _____ : the task-oriented dimension of marriage, including earning a living, spending money, and maintaining a household.

7. _____ : Marriage form in which one spouse, usually the husband, spends more time at paid work and the partner at unpaid work. In _____ marriages, one spouse, usually the wife, is doing the same amount of paid work but more unpaid work. The remaining marriages follow a _____ model.

8. _____: The premarital sexual standard that allows no premarital sex. The _____ standard allows it for men only; the _____ standard permits premarital sex for both women and men if there is a strong personal commitment; and the _____ standard approves of it for both men and women, even without love.

9. _____: descent traced unilaterally through the male line; a child is related only to the father's relatives.

10. _____: one woman married to two or more men; wife-sharing.

11. _____: a family consisting of one parent and one or more children.

12. _____: a family with one male and one female partner.

13. _____: marriage involving two or more men and two or more women.

14. _____: the residence pattern of couples who reside alone.

15. _____: marriage in which wife and husband have equal power.

16. _____: a family that includes more than spouses and unmarried children (e.g., grandparents, other relatives) living in the same residence.

17. _____: norm that marriage partners must be members of the same group.

18. _____: couple takes up residence with the wife's parents.

19. _____: marriage involving more than two partners.

20. _____: people related by blood or marriage.

21. _____: males are the formal head and ruling power in these families.

22. _____: descent that follows both the male and female lines; a child is related to relatives of both parents.

23. _____: family organization with an emphasis on biological relatedness (e.g., parents and children or brothers and sisters) rather than on the spousal relationship.

24. _____: marriage involving only two partners.

25._____: family form in which females are the formal head and ruling power.

26._____: two or more people related by blood, marriage, or adoption and residing together.

27._____: one man married to two or more women; husband-sharing.

28._____: descent traced unilaterally through the female line; a child is related only to the mother's relatives.

29._____: couple takes up residence with the husband's parents.

30._____: a family that includes only spouses and any unmarried children.

31._____: marriage between two people who are dissimilar in some important regard, such as religion, ethnicity, social class, personality, or age.

32._____: nuclear family including children from more than one union.

33._____: nuclear family with children from a prior union of one spouse.

34._____: a family with either two male or two female partners.

35._____: the norm that marriage partners must be chosen from outside a defined group.

SELF-QUIZ

1. Cohabitation is generally

   a) patriarchal
   b) matriarchal
   c) polygynous
   d) neolocal
   e) hedonistic

2. For a unit to be called a family, the people involved must

   a) customarily live in the same dwelling
   b) be related
   c) be related and customarily live in the same dwelling
   d) be related by marriage or common-law union
   e) include at least one person of each sex

3.   From anthropological data gathered in various societies, it is clear that only two types of marriage have been found with any frequency. They are

    a)   group marriage and polygyny
    b)   polygamy and monogamy
    c)   monogamy and group marriage
    d)   polygyny and polyandry
    e)   monogamy and polygyny

4.   In tribal societies

    a)   the nuclear family is generally paramount
    b)   reproduction is at a premium
    c)   the consanguine family is generally paramount
    d)   children are often spoiled
    e)   b and c

5.   Which of the following practices is the most uniform across societies?

    a)   acceptance of extra-marital intercourse
    b)   the incest taboo
    c)   discouragement of premarital intercourse
    d)   low premium on marriage
    e)   endogamy

6.   Which perspective looks at the family as one of the institutions of society and concentrates on instrumental exchanges?

    a)   symbolic interactionism
    b)   feminism
    c)   structural functionalism
    d)   social psychology
    e)   conflict theory

7.   What factor(s) most helped to decrease or change the functions previously performed by families?

    a)   a reduced influence of religion and a decline in the birth rate
    b)   industrialization
    c)   the women's liberation movement and reactions to it
    d)   the increase in the number of divorces
    e)   a and d

8.   The discussion about expressive exchanges concluded that
   a)   the family has kept most of its economic, political, and religious functions
   b)   the family has become a more important source of emotional gratification
   c)   families are more likely to stay together today than previously because they are a source of emotional gratification for individuals
   d)   families are now quicker to dissolve if a spouse finds the marriage not gratifying, a luxury unaffordable when families provided instrumental needs
   e)   b and d

9.   Since 1985, which has not increased?
   a)   divorce levels
   b)   births to mothers over age 30
   c)   post-marital cohabitation
   d)   remarriage
   e)   a and d

10.   Which standard of premarital sex received the greatest support among students?
   a)   love
   b)   abstinence
   c)   double
   d)   fun
   e)   all standards were equally supported

11.   Until the 1960s the _____ model of families saw a husband dependent on a wife for care of home and children and a wife dependent on a husband for income.
   a)   Victorian
   b)   expressive
   c)   macro
   d)   breadwinner
   e)   micro

12.   Higher income _____ a woman's chances for divorce. It _____ a man's.
   a)   decreases, increases
   b)   has no effect on, decreases
   c)   increases, decreases
   d)   increases, has no effect on
   e)   has no effect on, has no effect on

13.   Researchers see cohabitation today as increasingly
   a)   a form of trial marriage
   b)   a prelude to marriage
   c)   a way to avoid divorce
   d)   a substitute for marriage
   e)   a way to reduce STDs

14.   Which of the following statements is (are) false?

    a)   because of the burdens of child-rearing, marriages involving children have a higher divorce rate than childless unions

    b)   the younger the age at marriage, the greater the incidence of divorce

    c)   because they have already been hurt once, people entering second marriages have a lower divorce rate than those entering first marriages

    d)   from 1981 to 2001 the number of cohabiting couples more than doubled

    e)   a and c

15.   Which of the following statements is (are) true?

    a)   in the future, the institution of marriage may no longer exist

    b)   the proportion of married people in the population is almost as high as ever

    c)   childless couples will be the norm in the future

    d)   in most marriages, men and women are equal partners

    e)   a and c

FILL IN THE BLANKS

1.   Marriages preceded by cohabitation have _____ rates of dissolution than those in which the couple do not live together before marriage.

2.   Persons who customarily maintain a common residence but are not related form a _____ and not a family.

3.   Murdock's research showed that polyandry is rare and when it occurs it is often _____ who share a wife.

4.   Recent statistics indicate median ages of bride and groom at _____ and _____, respectively.

5.   Most individuals are motivated to marry and they have the potential ability. What they lack is _____.

6.   Concerning uniformity in family structure across societies, in most societies there is a high premium on _____. Another feature, almost uniform, is the incest taboo. Finally, the importance of _____ is found in most societies.

7.   The decade sometimes called the "golden age of the family" is the _____.

8.   What we are often seeing, rather than an empty nest, is adult children who still live at home, making it what some call a _____.

9.   In general, children of divorce tend to prefer living with a _____; second choice is a _____ not in a relationship and third a _____ who is.

10.   Non-industrial societies were held together by _____, that is, by the sense of identity people had with their communities. In the industrial world, societies are held together by _____, a division of labour that allows individuals to profit from the specialized abilities of others.

11.   While cohabitation used to be perceived as an alternative to being single, now it is more an alternative _____.

12.   Almost all lone parents leave this state within twenty years, about three-quarters to form new unions; for their children this raises the issue of a _____.

13.   In conversations about mate selection, two contradictory principles are heard: "opposites attract" and "like marries like." Which principle receives considerably more support? _____

14.   For both men and women _____ has become less central to the transition to the set of roles that define adult status.

15.   Parents of the baby boomers were the dutiful generation; their children more of a _____ generation.

16.   The _____ means that the less-involved person in a dating relationship has more power because of having less to lose if it ends.

Answers

KEY TERMS AND DEFINITIONS

1. mating gradient
2. expressive exchanges
3. homogamy
4. marriage
5. common-law union
6. instrumental exchanges
7. complementary-role, double-burden, collaborative or role-sharing
8. abstinence; double; love; fun
9. patrilineal
10. polyandry
11. lone-parent family
12. heterosexual family
13. group marriage
14. neolocal
15. equalitarian
16. extended family
17. endogamy
18. matrilocal
19. polygamy
20. kin
21. patriarchal
22. bilateral
23. consanguine family
24. monogamy
25. matriarchal
26. family
27. polygyny
28. matrilineal
29. patrilocal
30. nuclear family
31. heterogamy
32. blended family
33. reconstituted family
34. same-sex family
35. exogamy

SELF-QUIZ

1. d
2. c
3. e
4. e
5. b
6. c
7. b
8. e
9. e
10. a
11. d
12. c
13. d
14. e
15. b

FILL IN THE BLANKS

1. higher
2. household
3. brothers
4. 27, 29
5. knowledge of what is expected
6. marriage, inheritance
7. 1950s
8. cluttered nest
9. mother, father, mother
10. mechanical solidarity, organic solidarity
11. to being married
12. step-parent
13. like marries like
14. marriage
15. me
16. principle of least interest

CHAPTER 11

Religion

OBJECTIVES

1. To appreciate the rapidly secularizing and changing religious life of Canadians, one that may set us apart from our nearest neighbour.

2. To understand various analyses of religion and social change, looking at the work of Durkheim, Marx, and especially Weber, which emphasizes the Protestant ethic and its relation to the growth of capitalism.

3. To be able to compare and contrast different forms of religious organizations, including sect, church, denomination, ecclesia, and cult.

4. To know of the theory of religious economies and how it applies to North America.

5. To be aware of "invisible religion" and how it fits with contemporary movements to make religion more individualistic, tolerant, and pragmatic.

KEY TERMS AND DEFINITIONS

1. _____ : those things or experiences that appear to be inexplicable using the laws of nature and the material universe.

2. _____ : the attempt to reconcile and combine different philosophical and religious views, even some seemingly in conflict with each other.

3. _____ : the sociological term for religious organizations that are well-established, inclusive (open to all), and involve involuntary membership, usually from birth.

4. _____ : non-institutional and private expressions of religiosity in modern, largely secular societies.

5. _____ : objects and activities set apart by society and treated with awe and respect, often because of their association with gods.

6. _____ : removing the domination by religious institutions and symbols of other sectors of social life.

7. _____ : sense people have of sharing in the overall intellectual heritage and wisdom of their culture while also participating in religious rituals.

8. _____ : sense of excitement and power people experience when in a large crowd, such as a religious revival or rock concert.

9. _____ : the term for a very large, international religious organization that seeks to include everyone in its membership.

10. _____ : religious organization characterized by exclusivity, voluntary membership, a radical social outlook, and rigorous demands.

11. _____ : in a religious context, the idea that people are born with certain abilities in order to fulfill, through their life's work, God's will.

12. _____ : definition that uses what religion does, not what it is, as its primary criterion.

13. _____ : definition that uses some conception of what religion essentially is, some key characteristic, as its primary criterion.

14. _____ : literally, all that is not sacred; in most cases it is the world of everyday, non-religious experience.

15. _____ : a church that dominates a society and considers itself to be the sole legitimate religion of that society.

16. _____ : a system of beliefs and practices about transcendent things, and their nature and consequences for humanity.

17. _____ : practising self-discipline, especially doing without comforts, with a view to spiritual improvement.

18. _____ : belief that an all-knowing and all-powerful God determined, from the dawn of creation, who would be saved and who damned.

19. _____ : term used to describe the approach to work of some Protestants who perform their tasks with an unprecedented diligence and lack of concern for immediate material benefit.

20. _____ : a type of non-established religious organization, usually small, with a voluntary membership, and focused on the teachings of a charismatic leader.

21. _____ : church-like religious organizations that recognize the legitimacy of other religious groups with which they compete for members.

SELF-QUIZ

1.   Tylor's "belief in Spiritual Beings" is a _____ definition of religion.

    a) functional
    b) transcendent
    c) denominational
    d) substantive
    e) a, b, and c

2.   The _____ is a level, type, or dimension of reality thought to be intrinsically different from and in some sense higher than ordinary experience of the world.

    a) denominational
    b) ecclesiastic
    c) profane
    d) transcendent
    e) religious

3.   In his discussion of the Arunta, Durkheim noted how all aspects of their lives were divided into two categories. The _____ possesses a tremendous power and provides a kind of fixed point in reality around which all else circulates.

    a) miraculous
    b) totem
    c) sacred
    d) ritual
    e) emblem

4.   Up until about 5000 years ago the dominant form of religion in most of the world was

    a) ritualistic
    b) atheistic
    c) a Goddess religion
    d) agnostic
    e) pagan

5.   According to Weber, the spirit of capitalism was nourished by a combination of

    a) the accumulation of wealth and seeking of pleasure
    b) self-denial and the accumulation of wealth
    c) religious dogma and rational thinking
    d) the routinization of charisma and industrialization
    e) a and d

6.   For Weber, capitalism needed for its development Luther's idea of _____ and Calvin's idea of _____.

       a)   asceticism, reason
       b)   theses, fate
       c)   devotion, charisma
       d)   charisma, devotion
       e)   calling, predestination

7.   Jehovah's Witnesses are probably closest to which type of religious organization?

       a)   church
       b)   cult
       c)   sect
       d)   denomination
       e)   ecclesia

8.   Which of the following is true?

       a)   denominations very often become ecclesia
       b)   temples have been known to become sects
       c)   ecclesia often turn into cults
       d)   denominations often become cults
       e)   sects often become churches

9.   Organizations into which people are born and baptized as infants and whose membership is heterogeneous are called

       a)   cults
       b)   churches
       c)   sects
       d)   Pentecostals
       e)   mystical

10.   New religious consciousness is marked by all of the following except

       a)   tolerance for other religions
       b)   an emphasis on religious experience
       c)   revival and innovation
       d)   a suspicion of institutionalization
       e)   a holistic approach to life

11.   The rise of secular nationalism in Quebec and the decline in the power of the Roman Catholic Church came about largely as a result of

   a)   urbanization
   b)   mysticism
   c)   asceticism
   d)   increased church attendance
   e)   the Quiet Revolution

12.   Which is not one of Glock and Stark's eight dimensions of religious life?

   a)   ascetic
   b)   devotional
   c)   ritualistic
   d)   communal
   e)   belief

13.   To revive what it sees as the original or purer spirit, this splinter group breaks off from a denomination it sees as having accommodated to the world.

   a)   sect
   b)   cult
   c)   invisible religion
   d)   civil religion
   e)   both c and d

14.   _____ Canadians than Americans are religious, but they are _____ truly so.

   a)   More, less
   b)   More, much more
   c)   Fewer, more
   d)   Fewer, much less
   e)   There are no differences in the religious experiences of the two countries.

15.   For Stark et al., the most important product that religious firms market is the

   a)   indulgence
   b)   compensator
   c)   community
   d)   ritual
   e)   c and d

16.   In new religions, traditional dualities, such as God and humanity, spiritual and material, mind and body, are replaced by a(n)

   a)   invisible religion
   b)   pragmatism
   c)   mysticism
   d)   binary choice
   e)   holistic approach

FILL IN THE BLANKS

1.   A subtype in the church-sect typology, examples of _____ include Christian Science and Jehovah's Witnesses.

2.   Durkheim saw the origin of religious experience and the source of religious power not in God, but in _____ itself.

3.   Scientology was classified as a _____ in the discussion of types of religious organizations.

4.   _____ prophecies about the ultimate end of humankind may play an important role in cult suicides.

5.   The demonization of outsiders, the invention of crises, and the expelling of dissidents are used by leaders of cults to maintain their _____ authority.

6.   Except in Quebec, the _____ religion is doing better than others in not losing its weekly attendance at religious services.

7.   In 2006 the Ontario government made it clear that _____ would not join other faith-based arbitration; in fact the other forms would also be outlawed.

8.   Glock and Stark's _____ dimension measures the degree to which people think their religion is the one and only path to salvation.

9.   While the majority of Canadians believe in God, in 2001 one out of every _____ people claimed to have no religion.

10. Promises of reward at some later time or in some other place, or _____, comprise Stark and Bainbridge's fourth premise in their theory of religion.

11. Compared with other forms of Christianity, fundamentalist versions are based upon a more _____ interpretation of the Bible.

12. Dogmatism, ritualism, and hired clergy are characteristics of a _____.

13. The twentieth-century growth of Roman Catholic devotion in Ireland was closely tied to _____.

14. Wiccans and Neo-Pagans are contemporary adherents of _____. Many reject the reality of supernatural beings.

15. The transfer of authority from religion to economic, educational, medical, and other spheres is called _____, part of the secularization process.

Answers

KEY TERMS AND DEFINITIONS

1. supernatural
2. syncretism
3. church
4. invisible religion
5. sacred
6. secularization
7. collective conscience
8. collective effervescence
9. universal church
10. sect
11. calling
12. functionalist definition of religion
13. substantive definition of religion
14. profane
15. ecclesia
16. religion
17. ascetic
18. doctrine of predestination
19. vocation
20. cult
21. denomination

SELF-QUIZ

1. d
2. d
3. c
4. c
5. b
6. e
7. c
8. e
9. b
10. c
11. e
12. a
13. c
14. c
15. b
16. e

FILL IN THE BLANKS

1. established sects
2. society
3. cult
4. Apocalyptic
5. charismatic
6. Roman Catholic
7. Shariah law
8. particularistic
9. six
10. compensators
11. literal
12. church
13. Irish nationalism
14. witchcraft
15. institutional differentiation

CHAPTER 12

Media

OBJECTIVES

1. To understand the information revolution and its benefits and costs.

2. To learn how audiences react to the media, including how a cultural studies approach explains this topic.

3. To introduce research both on gender representation in the media and on media violence.

4. To be aware of the issues associated with the globalization of cyberspace for haves and have-nots.

KEY TERMS AND DEFINITIONS

1. _____: large corporations that either combine many different media holdings, or have interests both in media and other industrial sectors.

2. _____: school of research that focuses on how people create meaning in everyday life, sometimes in conflict with or resistant to the dominant values promoted by the major media.

3. _____: the use of computer networks such as the Internet in business, primarily by creating direct links between products and customers.

4. _____: the idea that viewing media violence encourages people to reduce their self-restraint and then commit real-life violence.

5. _____: idea that watching media violence, rather than stimulating real-life violence, provides a substitute or safety valve for it.

6. _____: a group of computer users separated geographically but linked together in cyberspace by shared interests and concerns.

7. _____: notion that audiences play a large role in interpreting or decoding media messages; often contrasted with the hypodermic model.

8. _____ : a critical term originally used to describe the crass, conservative, and conformist tendencies of commercial mass entertainment, now often used approvingly to refer to business-driven media.

9. _____ : the imaginary dimension in which we conceive of computer-mediated communication occurring.

10. _____ : tendency of international communications to create cultural mixes or crossovers between previously distinct national and/or ethnic groups.

11. _____ : the idea that heavy viewing of television leads people to perceive reality in ways consistent with what they see on TV shows.

12. _____ : the disparity between the capacities of the developed and less developed world to produce and distribute information.

13. _____ : the imposition of one nation's way of life on another, not through direct occupation but by indirect media influence.

14. _____ : a term for the tendency for repeated exposure to media violence to make people increasingly indifferent to, or accepting of, such incidents in real life.

15. _____ : the belief that media shoot powerful messages into weak, passive audiences, thus directly controlling their behaviour.

16. _____ : the idea that new technologies drive social change.

17. _____ : approach to communication studies focusing on the power relations governing the production, distribution, and consumption of information.

18. _____ : a new stage of civilization, supposedly created by computers and telecommunications, succeeding the old industrial society.

19. _____ : a phrase suggesting that computers and other digital technologies empower citizens by allowing them to create and circulate information for themselves.

SELF-QUIZ

1.   The countries most using the Internet (as a percent of population) generally are

   a)   in the Western hemisphere
   b)   resource poor
   c)   poor in other mass media forms
   d)   in the Third World
   e)   English-speaking nations

2.   In McLuhan's view, _____ was linked to rationality, linear thinking, and a split between the head and heart.

   a)   the oral tradition
   b)   radio
   c)   cyberspace
   d)   electronic media
   e)   print

3.   Bell's _____ society, which he said is propelled by advances in scientific knowledge, is roughly equivalent to the information society.

   a)   pre-industrial
   b)   post-industrial
   c)   industrial
   d)   global
   e)   none of the above

4.   In the Jihad versus McWorld debate, the former includes traditional _____ identity.

   a)   gender
   b)   nationalist
   c)   conspiracy
   d)   Shopping Network
   e)   a and d

5.   Attractive to the political right and left, the _____ model presents the audience as passive zombies or as glassy-eyed dupes.

   a)   effects
   b)   uses and gratification
   c)   hypodermic
   d)   cybernetic
   e)   cultural studies

6.   Men's style of television viewing, compared to that of women, is characterized by all of the following, except

    a)   systematic
    b)   silent
    c)   uninterrupted
    d)   unshared
    e)   watching while doing something else

7.   _____ exists where a corporation owns different stages or steps in a related economic process, such that companies with the same owner supply and consume each other's products.

    a)   A cartel
    b)   A virtual community
    c)   A transnational
    d)   Horizontal integration
    e)   Vertical integration

8.   More Canadians own a _____ than a telephone.

    a)   CD player
    b)   VCR
    c)   television
    d)   computer
    e)   DVD player

9.   Chomsky and Herman argued that five filters allow the U.S. media to control the thoughts of the populace; they do not include

    a)   "flak"
    b)   the Internet
    c)   mobilization against threats
    d)   a reliance on advertising as the primary income source
    e)   the dependency of the media on information provided by outside experts

10.   Video games, the fastest-growing segment of the current entertainment industry, also

    a)   have an estimated annual value of $10 trillion
    b)   are the primary source of adolescent violence
    c)   are the primary source of hybridization
    d)   rake in more money than the Hollywood box office
    e)   are the primary source of information imbalance

FILL IN THE BLANKS

1.   According to McLuhan, television, with its immediacy and intimacy, retribalizes humankind but on a planetary scale, creating the _____.

2.   Some talk about the post-industrial society, some about network society, and some about web society. But the most common term is the _____ society.

3.   Political economists are concerned because, despite the multiplicity of media outlets, all transmit a common corporate-speak that depicts an air-brushed _____ while at the same time hiding issues of injustice.

4.   Porn, hate speech, and viruses are hard to fight because of the _____ nature of the Internet, which makes them difficult to police.

5.   Cultural studies includes the concept of audience _____, not just the encoding of the products of mass communication.

6.   _____ were structured to fit the rhythm of housework, scheduled to punctuate the day, but designed to allow distracted viewing.

7.   Long, vicious harangues in online discussion groups are called _____.

8.   While "sex sells," it is just as important that _____, a fact that may lead to more equitable treatment of women and sexual minorities.

9.   _____ is associated with a shift to a service economy, a move from manual to technical jobs, and increased capacities to forecast social change.

10.   The _____doll was used to examine the effects of viewing violence.

11.   Our lives are increasingly _____, more reliant on technically sophisticated, socially organized communications that convey, filter, and construct our experience.

12.   The placeless, global consumer capitalism is also referred to as _____. It squeezes out any form of cultural production that is not for sale.

13.   Some fear that the new virtual world will change people from couch potatoes to _____.

14.   _____ is a term from Gibson, the Canadian science-fiction author.

15.   Users of the Internet tend to be drawn from some groups and not from others; _____ and _____ are generally under-represented.

Answers

KEY TERMS AND DEFINITIONS

1. communications conglomerates
2. cultural studies school
3. virtual commerce
4. disinhibition
5. surrogate theory
6. virtual community
7. active audience theory
8. culture industry
9. cyberspace
10. hybridization

11. cultivation effect
12. information imbalance
13. cultural imperialism
14. desensitization
15. hypodermic model
16. technological determinism
17. political economy of media
18. information society
19. technologies of freedom

SELF-QUIZ

1. e
2. e
3. b
4. b

5. c
6. e
7. e
8. c

9. b
10. d

FILL IN THE BLANKS

1. global village
2. information
3. happy consumerism
4. transnational
5. decoding
6. Soaps
7. flame wars
8. "money talks"

9. Post-industrialism
10. Bobo
11. "mediated"
12. McWorld
13. mouse potatoes
14. Cyberspace
15. women, the poor

CHAPTER 13

Education

OBJECTIVES

1. To understand the central functions of education and its two different curricula, the formal and the hidden.

2. To appreciate a conflict view of education and the class bias found in most educational systems, for example, streaming.

3. To be aware of some of the other problems of schooling: bullying, sexual harassment, and other types of violence.

4. To understand historical and current attempts at educational reform, including their underlying rationales and challenges to implementation.

KEY TERMS AND DEFINITIONS

1. _____ : the personal knowledge and skills one can use to understand and manipulate the dominant culture of society.

2. _____ : a mismatch between the skills, knowledge, and abilities one acquires in school and the lesser ones actually required on the job.

3. _____ : educational practice based upon the belief that students learn better when they are grouped with their academic peers.

4. _____ : means that people's social environment, including cultural capital, makes them see the world in a certain way, which then leads them to act, perceive, and think in a certain way.

5. _____ : looks at how education can become a catalyst for social change and greater empowerment, for example, through a deconstruction of schooling.

6. _____ : what schools teach explicitly, for example, reading, writing, and math.

7. _____ : principle that people are selected for social positions based on achievement and in accordance with universal standards, such as talent, tenacity, and hard work.

8. _____: propose a direct relationship between educational attainment and labour market outcomes; more education means better jobs.

9. _____: the view that many working-class students are not victims of the school, but have actively rejected the middle-class values there and embraced the value of manual labour (based on a study involving "lads").

10. _____: a catch-phrase; an extension of education now made necessary by the ever-changing skills needed for the new knowledge economy.

11. _____: a consequence, such as dropping out of school, of the fact that some students feel alienated at school, and do not see their experiences reflected in the curriculum.

12. _____: concept that the requirements for entry into some occupations have increased although the job requirements have not.

13. _____: part of schooling through which one learns the informal knowledge required for a smoother everyday life.

14. _____: an individualistic view, it proposes that people make those decisions that they predict will maximize the returns on their investments in education.

15. _____: the view that the roles required by the workplace determine what will be taught at school; as roles change, schooling must change.

SELF-QUIZ

1. The unemployment rate in 2000 for those with less than a high school education is about _____ that of those who have gone to university.

   a) twice
   b) three times
   c) equal to
   d) just under
   e) four times

2. Internships, co-op placements, and youth apprenticeship programs are created to increase

   a) rational choices
   b) human capital
   c) cultural integration
   d) *habitus*
   e) critical pedagogy

3.   On average about _____ of the bystanders will help the victim of a schoolyard bully. A more usual response is to do nothing or even to join forces with the bully.

    a) 95%
    b) one
    c) three-quarters
    d) half
    e) a quarter

4.   Students who are athletic, good looking, and comfortably well-off are generally popular in high school and unlikely to

    a) be called "grits"
    b) be jocks
    c) have much cultural capital
    d) be streamed to lower-ability math classes
    e) this question cannot be answered without more information on their intelligence

5.   Which country below is the most egalitarian, that is, has the smallest gap between rich and poor students in reading literacy? For question 6, using the same list, which country is the least?

    a) Canada
    b) United States
    c) Sweden
    d) France
    e) Germany

6.   See 5. _____

7.   In Germany the diploma required by students in order to enter university comes from the

    a) *Hauptschule*
    b) *Gymnasium*
    c) *Realschule*
    d) for boys, a and for girls, b (above)
    e) for boys, b and for girls, a (above).

8.   German students, unlike those in Canada, experience their first formal streaming after Grade

    a) 1
    b) 4
    c) 7
    d) 9
    e) 11

9.   Anyon argued that lower-class students experience all of the following in their school except

    a)   memorizing facts
    b)   rule following
    c)   few explanations for classroom activities
    d)   rote learning
    e)   negotiating

10.   Bowles and Gintis argued that upper-class students are taught all of the following except

    a)   cleanliness
    b)   leadership
    c)   problem solving
    d)   critical thinking
    e)   actually, they argued that the students are taught a, b, c, and d

11.   The term Willis used for the boys who would skip school, not do their homework, fight, and threaten their teachers is

    a)   Borstal boys
    b)   lads
    c)   the disenchanted and disaffected
    d)   crusaders
    e)   the future elite criminals of Britain

12.   Which of the following is not a goal of ethnocentric schools?

    a)   making it easier for students to make the transition to inclusive schools
    b)   creating a safer school environment
    c)   the teaching of ethnic pride
    d)   appreciating different learning styles
    e)   increasing self-confidence of ethnic minority students

13.   _____ argue that people do not inherit their adult roles but instead achieve them through open competition in the school system.

    a)   Functionalists
    b)   Marxists
    c)   School principals
    d)   School subcultures
    e)   Critical pedagogues

14.   Which province had the lowest reading scores in Canada and which the highest?

    a)   New Brunswick, Alberta
    b)   Saskatchewan, Ontario
    c)   Newfoundland, British Columbia
    d)   Quebec, Alberta
    e)   Prince Edward Island, Ontario

15.   People with less than or just a high school diploma earn _____ percent of what university graduates do.

    a)   10
    b)   25
    c)   50
    d)   60
    e)   it really depends on the university

FILL IN THE BLANKS

1.   It is the students from the _____ class who want their learning to be immediately applicable and have relevance for their chosen career paths.

2.   In some U.S. schools the use of _____ has been added; they feel like having your funny bone banged 17 times a second for five seconds.

3.   That Ontario Scholars (those with a high school graduating average of at least 80 percent) have gone from a very rare to a common phenomenon over time is another example of _____.

4.   It is through the _____ curriculum that students are exposed to what they will experience as employees, parents, and in other adult roles.

5.   Fewer than 20 percent of women have broken through the _____ to become top business executives.

6.   A budget cut that hurts already disadvantaged schools the most is an example of _____ violence.

7.   When children's performance in school is based on the subjective labels applied to them by teachers in Grades 1 and 2, rather than on their actual abilities, it is called a _____.

8.   _____ status represents dominant forms of gender identity, masculinity, and heterosexuality.

9.   The children who side with and even join the bully are more likely to be _____ and _____.

10.   It is estimated that almost one in three Americans in their mid-twenties is a _____, most of them coming from poor and working-class families.

Answers

KEY TERMS AND DEFINITIONS

1. cultural capital
2. underemployment
3. streaming
4. habitus
5. critical pedagogy
6. formal curriculum
7. meritocracy
8. human capital theories
9. resistance theory
10. lifelong learning
11. symbolic violence
12. credential inflation
13. hidden curriculum
14. rational choice theory
15. correspondence theory

SELF-QUIZ

1. b
2. b
3. e
4. a
5. a
6. e
7. b
8. b
9. e
10. a
11. b
12. a
13. a
14. a
15. c

FILL IN THE BLANKS

1. working
2. tasers
3. credential inflation
4. hidden
5. glass ceiling
6. state
7. self-fulfilling prophecy
8. Jock
9. older and male
10. college dropout

CHAPTER 14

Organizations and Work

OBJECTIVES

1. To grasp a new definition of the human activity called work, and examine its effect upon people. How is it different from non-human work?

2. To appreciate the evolution of the organization of work, including distinctions between social and detailed divisions of labour and formal and informal organization.

3. To understand the meanings that work has for workers and how these vary by gender, ethnicity, and age.

4. To illustrate some of the current trends and issues in work.

KEY TERMS AND DEFINITIONS

1. _____ : the process by which a company reduces its labour force in order to reduce operating costs.

2. _____ : working not for the enjoyment of the job, but for the money that then translates into life enjoyment.

3. _____ : Michels' idea that the leadership of even democratic organizations becomes elitist; rule by the many becomes rule by the few.

4. _____ : a system that seeks to transfer control of the work process from the workers to the managers and owners. It is built upon a detailed division of labour that is perceived of as leading to "efficiency."

5. _____ : breaking a task down into sub-tasks which are then given to different people who can be more easily trained and paid less than a multi-skilled person who might perform the whole task.

6. _____ : assembly-line process of mass production that facilitates mass consumption, so named because of its developer.

7. _____ : the socially sanctioned understanding that if people work hard and produce more goods and services each year, the economy will grow, benefiting all financially, both workers and owners.

8. _____: division of jobs among people to ensure the survival of society and its prosperity.

9. _____: a special type of formal organization characterized by written rules and a hierarchical authority; it emphasizes impersonal work relationships, technical knowledge, and rationality.

10. _____: marked by a division of labour and set up to achieve a goal or goals, examples include hospitals and political parties.

11. _____: as developed by Marx, it describes the separation of workers from the product of their labour, as well as from the process of work, their fellow workers, and even their basic humanity.

12. _____: the rules and structures that arise to meet the challenges of the complex day-to-day life in formal organizations.

13. _____: current practice in which companies now look worldwide for the most profitable place to set up their operations.

14. _____: process of forming unions, reaching collective agreements, and solving the disputes that arise when management and labour cannot agree.

15. _____: associations in a definable workplace, representing a group of workers in their negotiations with an employer to get a contract.

16. _____: making materials or mental constructs more useful to the producer.

17. _____: workplace actions aimed at passively or actively slowing, reversing, avoiding, or protesting management directions and strategies.

18. _____: term used to describe the fact that people in different social categories do different types of work.

19. _____: a process where the principles of fast-food restaurants become more widespread, including low pay and little full-time work.

20. _____: worker activities aimed at disrupting the flow of production.

21. _____: Weber's term for the overriding concern of capitalist society to constantly increase efficiency; it includes rules and a division of labour.

SELF-QUIZ

1. Worker resistance to change is more likely when the following occur, except

    a) they do not understand what is going on
    b) their security is jeopardized
    c) changes have been forced upon them
    d) they have no stake in the new system
    e) the informal organization has become bureaucratized

2. Rumours and temporary agreements mark the _____ aspect of organization.

    a) bureaucratic
    b) formal
    c) informal
    d) complex division of labour
    e) industrial

3. That which distinguishes human work from that performed by animals is human

    a) division of labour
    b) class consciousness
    c) greater rationality
    d) ability to conceptualize
    e) skill

4. _____ theorists point out that individuals create temporary agreements and informal understandings with co-workers to facilitate the completion of their jobs.

    a) Informal organization
    b) Formal organization
    c) Marxist
    d) Negotiated order
    e) Symbolic interactionist

5. Durkheim's term for the condition arising from a division of labour that leaves people feeling atomized and experiencing normlessness is

    a) charisma
    b) anomie
    c) mechanical solidarity
    d) organic solidarity
    e) alienation

6. Women's most frequent job is in childcare; for men it is as

    a) longshore workers
    b) machinists, metalworkers, and woodworkers
    c) cleaners
    d) retail salespersons and clerks
    e) motor vehicle and transit drivers

7.   Which of the following is not a characteristic of Weber's concept of bureaucracy and better thought of as anti-bureaucratic?

a)   expert training
b)   hierarchy
c)   flexible rules
d)   written documents
e)   careers

8.   Michels' main reason(s) for the tendency toward oligarchy is (are)

a)   a monopoly on the knowledge needed to run a bureaucracy
b)   a need of workers to be motivated more by social than by economic rewards
c)   an increase in altruism
d)   a and b
e)   a and c

9.   Which could be most accused of manipulating workers?

a)   Taylorism
b)   Fordism
c)   Total Quality Management and Continuous Quality Improvement
d)   bureaucratic theory
e)   scientific management

10.   Canada's social contract is in trouble for several reasons, but not because of

a)   free trade agreements
b)   globalization of production
c)   reduction in government spending
d)   the increasingly detailed division of labour
e)   b and c only

11.   Unemployment in Canada is increasing, but not because of

a)   greater power in the informal organization
b)   the decline of mass production here
c)   the movement of jobs to Third World countries
d)   the reduction in the civil service
e)   c and d

12.   Lower today, Canada in the 1990s had close to ___ percent official unemployment, although it did vary by region.

a)   10
b)   20
c)   2
d)   5
e)   30

13.   The theoretical foundation of negotiated order theory is found in

    a)   ethnomethodology
    b)   functionalism
    c)   symbolic interactionism
    d)   conflict theory
    e)   the writings of Durkheim

14.   McDonaldization involves all of the following except

    a)   calculability
    b)   control
    c)   predictability
    d)   social contract
    e)   a standardization leading to efficiency

FILL IN THE BLANKS

1.   Rumour mills remind us that informal networks are not always positive but can be _____ as well.

2.   According to Pareto, _____ eventually turn into lions and the circulation of elites cycle repeats itself.

3.   Compared to animals, human creation is based on _____ not _____.

4.   Weber saw bureaucracies as marking the growth of _____ society, one based on law and reason.

5.   In hunting and gathering societies, families divided jobs by gender, called a _____ division of labour.

6.   According to Marx, _____ is a structural problem, rooted in the relationship between the managers and the managed, the deciders and the doers.

7.   The _____ of the 1930s was the impetus for a social contract.

8.   _____ was the British economist on whose idea the social contract is based.

9.   They are radical, rely heavily on the informal organization, increasingly subject to McDonaldization, and we literally cannot live without them: _____.

10.   Involving workers in the decision-making process was more successful in Japan than in Canada because their society is more _____; here we have more distrust.

11.   They have lost full-time employment, their wages are going down, and they are the most frequent group to be hurt on the job; they are_____.

12.   The _____ thesis argues that the human ability to use tools in the process of work develops the human capacity for conceptualization that leads to more work with tools, etc.

13.   Taylor argued that all _____ must be removed from the shop floor and placed in the hands of management.

14.   The four letters of the alphabet, heard weekly, that typify instrumentalism are _____; employers would prefer to hear TGIM.

15.   It is the _____ problem that is foremost on the agenda for those interested in the study of work today.

Answers

KEY TERMS AND DEFINITIONS

1. downsizing
2. instrumentalism
3. iron law of oligarchy
4. scientific management
5. detailed division of labour
6. Fordism
7. social contract
8. social division of labour
9. bureaucracy
10. formal organizations
11. alienation
12. informal organization
13. globalization of production
14. industrial relations
15. unions
16. work
17. resistance
18. occupational segregation
19. McDonaldization
20. sabotage
21. rationalization

SELF-QUIZ

1. e
2. c
3. a
4. d
5. b
6. e
7. c
8. a
9. c
10. d
11. a
12. a
13. c
14. d

FILL IN THE BLANKS

1. dysfunctional
2. foxes
3. learning, instinct
4. legal rational
5. social
6. alienation
7. Great Depression
8. John Maynard Keynes
9. nurses
10. collectivist
11. youth
12. Washburn
13. brainwork
14. TGIF
15. lack-of-work

CHAPTER 15

Social Movements

OBJECTIVES

1. To understand the meaning of the general term "collective behaviour" and its specific forms: panics, crowds, fads, crazes, publics, and social movements.

2. To understand the collective behaviour perspective on social movements, including Blumer's work and emergent norm theory.

3. To compare and contrast other theoretical perspectives on social movements—the social breakdown approach, the relative deprivation approach, the collective action approaches, and postmodernism and the new social movement approach.

4. To be aware of the principal cleavages and integrative bonds that have shaped collective action in Canada, with emphasis on regional and ethnic cleavages.

KEY TERMS AND DEFINITIONS

1. _____ : activity in which a large number of people do not accept some of the prevailing values and norms. Behaviour of this kind may be described as less "institutionalized" than ordinary behaviour.

2. _____ : a large and dispersed group made up of persons who share an interest. They may hold similar views about it, or sharply disagree.

3. _____ : large collectivities of people either seeking or resisting social change; sociologists often assume that they are the most institutionalized form of collective behaviour.

4. _____ : created when a rational calculation of self-interest persuades one not to engage in collective action, letting others do the work.

5. _____ : a set of beliefs providing the basis for collective action; it identifies a problem, diagnoses it, attributes blame, offers a solution, and facilitates the co-ordination of activities, directing them toward a common goal.

6. _____ : the attachment of individuals to social groups or institutions.

7. _____: an explanation of crowd behaviour that stresses not only diversity of membership but also a perception of consensus that leads to a new norm expressing the apparent will of the crowd.

8. _____: an approach to collective behaviour that argues that social unrest occurs when established institutions are disrupted or weakened.

9. _____: the rapid and uncontrolled spread of a mood, impulse, or form of conduct through a collectivity of people.

10. _____: groups in which people come together for specific purposes, such as feminist organizations or pensioners' associations.

11. _____: a movement in the 1960s in Quebec to expand governmental powers, to decrease church power, to modernize Quebec, and to fight vigorously for *la survivance.*

12. _____: the pursuit of goals by more than one person; as an explanation of social movements, it looks at integration and cleavage factors and seeks to explain variations in social movements over time.

13. _____: transfer of resources, particularly human resources, used to pursue a goal or set of goals to the pursuit of another goal or set of goals.

14. _____: a special kind of fad requiring intense commitment and enthusiasm and regarded as strange, even offensive, by others.

15. _____: a division (based on age, class, or ethnicity, etc.) that may result in the formation of distinct social groups.

16. _____: temporary group of people in close physical proximity; only the unconventional type is included as a form of collective behaviour.

17. _____: a set of beliefs or principles that helps people to interpret and explain their world and may provide a basis for collective action.

18. _____: an unconventional practice that spreads rapidly and is adopted in a short period of time by a large number of people; a social norm.

19. _____: difference between what people believe they have a right to receive (*expectations*) and what they actually receive (their *achievements*).

20. _____: an immediate course of action that occurs when people are afraid and try to save themselves or their property from perceived danger.

21. _____: the survival of French Canada as a distinct society.

22._____ : the personal benefits an individual can derive from belonging to an association or by joining a social movement; they help to motivate.

23._____ : the domination of a class or classes over others, not only economically, but politically and culturally as well.

24._____ : enduring communities that have lived together over long periods of time, sharing language, culture, and other attributes.

SELF-QUIZ

1.   Postmodernists reject all of the following except

    a)   meta-narratives
    b)   positivism
    c)   totalistic theory
    d)   indeterminacy
    e)   Marx

2.   The voiceless are most likely to get attention from those who adopt a _____ approach.

    a)   cleavage
    b)   postmodern
    c)   relative deprivation
    d)   rising expectations
    e)   social integration

3.   Blumer's idea of social contagion said that the fundamental process missing in crowd behaviour is

    a)   rationality
    b)   panic
    c)   a common enemy
    d)   circular reaction
    e)   c and d only

4.   Which of the following does not describe "new social movements"?

    a)   social breakdown
    b)   anti-authority
    c)   less emphasis on the economy than in older movements
    d)   a concern with values and culture
    e)   spontaneity and decentralization

5. Who is Scotland's most famous outlaw?

   a) Duncan
   b) Guy Fawkes
   c) Rob Roy
   d) Robin Hood
   e) Robert Carlyle

6. Bourassa thought the primary mission of French Canadians was to preserve their

   a) language
   b) culture
   c) religion
   d) institutions
   e) economy

7. Which of the following is a criticism of the collective behaviour tradition?

   a) too much attention is given to social structure
   b) too little attention is spent on interest groups and the conflicts among them
   c) too much attention is given to mobilization factors
   d) ignoring the distinguishing aspect of social movements, that is the lack of institutionalization
   e) none of the above

8. According to the collective action perspective, two kinds of factors are necessary for the occurrence of social movements; they are

   a) social breakdown and relative deprivation
   b) discontent and consensus
   c) cleavage and integrating
   d) mobilization and discontent
   e) social breakdown and social isolation

9. De Tocqueville thought that a major factor underlying the French Revolution was

   a) rising expectations
   b) discontent
   c) dissatisfaction
   d) circular reaction
   e) contagion

10.   Social cleavage between regions, combined with social integration within regions, has resulted in collective action that tends to be weak and divided
_____, while often strong _____.

a)   nationally, regionally
b)   regionally, nationally
c)   individually, socially
d)   politically, economically
e)   b and d

11.   Nationally, the Progressive Movement did not survive long as a political force

a)   because it relied too heavily on religious broadcasts to attract followers
b)   because its leader died and the routinization of charisma failed
c)   because it was too local, strong primarily in the Prairie provinces
d)   because it was taken over by the CCF
e)   b and c

12.   Which political party charged business elites in the east with controlling and manipulating the Canadian economy to serve their own interests?

a)   CCF
b)   NDP
c)   Social Credit
d)   Communist
e)   none of the above

13.   Marxists have generally supported a _____ approach.

a)   collective action
b)   postmodern
c)   relative deprivation
d)   emergent norm
e)   social movement

14.   The section on mobilization pointed out that many social movements collapse merely because they lack

a)   steam
b)   money
c)   cleavage factors
d)   integrating factors
e)   advancement opportunities for new recruits

15.   Nationalism has long been popular among the Québécois. Before the Quiet Revolution, the survival of French Canada was to be achieved by

    a)   advocating separation from the rest of Canada
    b)   keeping people loyal to traditional values
    c)   strengthening ties with France
    d)   accepting the processes of urbanization and industrialization
    e)   maintaining tight control over the provincial government

FILL IN THE BLANKS

1.   Historically _____, not oppression, has been the most important cultural basis for social movements.

2.   The criterion for belonging to a _____ is not a blood tie or common ancestor, but instead a common name.

3.   According to social breakdown theory, _____, _____, and _____ individuals are those most likely to participate in social unrest.

4.   Collective action theorists argue that it is more important to study the _____ rather than the *amount* of social unrest and how it differs historically and in different places.

5.   The two revolts of interest to Marxists are those that led to the overthrow of _____, called bourgeois revolts, and those that Marx hoped would lead to the overthrow of _____.

6.   The theory that best explains why many different people would begin to believe in something, such as a need to recycle or to take echinacea, is _____.

7.   The English do not call their overthrow of Charles I in the seventeenth century a revolution but instead call it the _____.

8.   There is a widespread supposition in sociological writings that social unrest occurs when established institutions are _____.

9.   One of the significant contributions of Gramsci was to persuade Marxists of the importance of _____ struggles against the existing order.

10.   People like Henri Bourassa are called _____ because they believed both in independence from Great Britain and provincial autonomy.

11.   Collective _____ refers to relatively non-institutionalized conduct, that is, conduct that departs from the ordinary and routine. In contrast, collective _____ covers both institutionalized and non-institutionalized activity.

12.   The major _____ include student, urban, feminist, environmental, and gay and lesbian varieties.

13.   We learn about the views of a _____ by studying the results of political elections, calls to phone-in shows, letters to newspapers, etc.

14.   The "Regina Manifesto" is associated with the _____ political party.

15.   Those patterns of differentiation that have had the most effect on collective action in Canada are _____, _____, _____, _____, _____, _____, and _____.

Answers

KEY TERMS AND DEFINITIONS

1. collective behaviour
2. public
3. social movements
4. free-rider problem
5. ideology
6. social integration
7. emergent norm theory
8. social breakdown approach
9. social contagion
10. status blocs
11. Quiet Revolution
12. collective action
13. mobilization
14. craze
15. social cleavage
16. crowd
17. frame
18. fad
19. relative deprivation
20. panic
21. *la survivance*
22. selective incentives
23. hegemony
24. status communities

SELF-QUIZ

1. d
2. b
3. a
4. a
5. c
6. c
7. b
8. c
9. a
10. a
11. c
12. c
13. a
14. b
15. b

FILL IN THE BLANKS

1. religion
2. clan
3. alienated, uprooted, socially maladjusted
4. character
5. feudalism, capitalism
6. emergent norm theory
7. English Civil War
8. disrupted or weakened
9. non-economic, including ideological
10. dual nationalists
11. behaviour, action
12. new social movements
13. public
14. CCF
15. age, class, ethnicity, region, rural or urban residence, gender, sexual orientation

CHAPTER 16

Demography and Urbanization

OBJECTIVES

1. To learn the basic variables of population study—fertility, mortality, and migration—and the part each plays, in conjunction with other social, cultural, and economic factors in social life.

2. To understand several theoretical perspectives on population change—demographic transition theory and the views of Malthus and Marx.

3. To be aware of different measures of mortality, fertility, and migration, and to know their correlates in the Canadian context, past and present.

4. To appreciate patterns of urbanization in the developed and developing world.

KEY TERMS AND DEFINITIONS

1. _____: measure for the average number of children a woman (or group of women) will have in a lifetime.

2. _____: indicators that measure demographic behaviour during a particular time period, such as a year or decade.

3. _____: a measure derived from a life table estimating the average life span for persons exposed to a given set of age-specific death rates.

4. _____: Malthus's term for those occurrences, such as war, famine, and disease, that reduce overpopulation.

5. _____: a measure based on the ratio of persons under 15 plus those over 65 to those in the working ages 15–64.

6. _____: a measure of childbearing rates computed by dividing the number of births to women of a particular age group by the total number of women in that age group.

7. _____: movement across legally defined boundaries; within a country it is called _____ while crossing a country's border makes it _____.

8. _____: a fertility measure computed by dividing the number of births in a time period by the size of the total population.

9. _____: (Malthus's) checks to overpopulation, such as abstinence and later marriage, which reduce the number of conceptions.

10. _____: the idea that populations pass through a three-stage process, from relatively high fertility and mortality levels, to high fertility but low mortality, and finally to low fertility and low mortality.

11. _____: a measure of population growth based on the difference between the crude birth rate and the crude death rate.

12. _____: measure of mortality that divides the number of deaths of people of a particular age by the total number of people of that age.

13. _____: the academic discipline that studies population processes.

14. _____: mortality measure computed by dividing the number of deaths in a time period by the total population.

15. _____: graph showing proportions of the population in age–sex categories.

16. _____: indicators that measure behaviour, over time, of people who share a common starting point, such as year of birth or date of marriage.

17. _____: a statistical model, based upon the probability of dying at given ages, estimating the average number of years of life remaining for persons of varying ages.

SELF-QUIZ

1. To grasp the magnitude of world population growth, remember that every three weeks the world adds to its population numbers equal to the size of _____.

   a) Regina
   b) Mexico City
   c) Toronto
   d) Vancouver
   e) Fredericton

2. Stage one of the demographic transition is characterized by

   a) high fertility, low mortality
   b) low fertility, low mortality
   c) high fertility, high mortality
   d) low fertility, high mortality
   e) none of the above

3.   Today's developing nations are at a disadvantage in trying to duplicate Europe's experience with the demographic transition because

   a)   the decrease in mortality occurred too quickly for them to adjust
   b)   of a dramatic increase in fertility but no corresponding increase in mortality
   c)   new methods of birth control are required now
   d)   they are stuck in stage one of the demographic transition
   e)   they prefer positive to preventive checks

4.   Malthus based his ideas on the relationship of population to the social and economic world. Which of the following could not be one of his arguments?

   a)   population invariably increases when the means of subsistence increase
   b)   new forms of male birth control are needed to keep population in check
   c)   population is necessarily limited by the means of subsistence
   d)   checks to population growth include vice, war, and famine
   e)   a and c

5.   While about half of Canadians change their residence at least once during a five-year period, _____ percent move to a different province.

   a)   60
   b)   50
   c)   33
   d)   25
   e)   5

6.   Which of the following is a criticism of Malthus's theory of overpopulation?

   a)   overestimating the advances the Agricultural Revolutions in food production
   b)   defining the level of subsistence too specifically
   c)   he would and could not foresee the widespread application of birth control
   d)   placing too much attention on capitalist structure rather than on individual initiative
   e)   b and d

7.   While the rates of natural increase in Europe never surpassed 2 percent, in some developing countries today it has hit _____ percent, doubling every 17 years.

   a)   40
   b)   30
   c)   20
   d)   10
   e)   4

8.   Arguing that single people die earlier than married because of the factors that encouraged them not to marry in the first place is the _____ hypothesis.

   a)   selection
   b)   conflict
   c)   functional
   d)   evolutionary
   e)   positive checks

9.   Which country is the near-perfect example of demographic transition theory?

   a)   Thailand
   b)   China
   c)   Mexico
   d)   India
   e)   South Korea

10.   Which of the following individuals (of equal age) is likely to die first?

   a)   a married male from a middle socioeconomic status
   b)   a divorced female of French origin
   c)   a single male from a lower socioeconomic status
   d)   a married female from a lower socioeconomic status
   e)   a divorced male from a middle socioeconomic status

11.   Which continent is home to more of the largest cities in the world than the others?

   a)   South America
   b)   North America
   c)   Europe
   d)   Africa
   e)   Asia

12.   Which was not a major cause of mortality decline in Western countries?

   a)   better nutrition
   b)   modern medicine
   c)   better sanitation
   d)   an improved standard of living
   e)   a, c, and d

13.   The world's crude birth rate today is about

   a)   38
   b)   28
   c)   21
   d)   13
   e)   3

14. In Western societies, which of the following has the greatest, if perhaps unintended, effect on fertility?

 a) breastfeeding
 b) abstinence
 c) marriage patterns; later marriage reduces fertility
 d) migration
 e) urbanization

15. A population pyramid

 a) provides information on the average number of years any individual can expect to live upon reaching a certain age
 b) can reveal if a society has an old or a young population
 c) allows a study of population in terms of distribution, composition, and change
 d) gives information pertaining to the internal migration of people
 e) gives information pertaining to the number of neonatal and perinatal deaths per year in a population

FILL IN THE BLANKS

1. Demography's primary variables are _____, _____, and _____.

2. _____ refers to the biological potential to bear children, not to actual childbearing .

3. It is clear that population growth on a world scale is a function of the relationship between only two things: _____ and _____.

4. Stages two and three of the demographic transition can be summarized as follows:

 Stage two: _____ fertility + _____ mortality = _____ increase.

 Stage three: _____ fertility + _____ mortality = _____ increase.

5. While as late as 1960 births to unmarried mothers were about 4 percent of the total, today the figure is closer to _____ percent, and in Quebec double that.

6. Malthus was not only a demographer but a _____.

7.   Between 1972 and 2000 the largest provincial gainer of internal migrants was
      _____.

8.   Most immigrants to Canada do not go to the empty lands of the West but to
      _____, _____, and _____.

9.   Overall, more than _____ of Canada's population lives on a small percentage
      of its land, specifically in the Windsor–Quebec City corridor.

10.   _____ determinants of fertility include abortion, contraception,
      and breastfeeding.

11.   A _____, not industrialization or transportation, was the most basic
      factor that allowed the initial growth of cities and urbanization.

12.   For sexually active unmarried women, _____ is the most common
      form of contraception (condom use is increasing), while for married people it is
      _____.

13.   Simon beat Ehrlich in their debate, with a final score of _____ to _____ for
      decreasing prices of the five commodities.

14.   A good _____ system is the main factor that allows the growth of
      suburbs on vacant land on a city's borders.

15.   Children of the baby boom generation are called the _____ generation.

16.   All people who share a common starting point, such as being born in the 1980s,
      are part of a particular _____.

Answers

KEY TERMS AND DEFINITIONS

1. total fertility rate
2. period measures
3. expectation of life at birth
4. positive checks
5. dependency ratio
6. age-specific fertility rates
7. migration, internal migration, international migration
8. crude birth rate (CBR)
9. preventive checks
10. demographic transition theory
11. rate of natural increase
12. age-specific death rates
13. demography
14. crude death rate (CDR)
15. population pyramid
16. cohort measures
17. life table

SELF-QUIZ

1. c
2. c
3. a
4. b
5. e
6. c
7. e
8. a
9. e
10. c
11. e
12. b
13. c
14. c
15. b

FILL IN THE BLANKS

1. fertility, mortality, migration
2. Fecundity
3. fertility, mortality
4. high, low, rapid; low, low, slow
5. 30
6. minister
7. Alberta
8. Toronto, Vancouver, and Montreal
9. half
10. Proximate
11. food surplus
12. the pill, sterilization
13. five, zero
14. transportation
15. echo
16. cohort

CHAPTER 17

Social Change

OBJECTIVES

1.   To understand how human societies have changed over the past 10 000 years, from gathering and hunting to post-industrial societies.

2.   To be familiar with theories of social change: evolutionism, the Weber thesis, developmental theories, historical materialism, and state theory of modernization.

3.   To learn something about specific changes, including greater equality, the decline of the traditional family, postmodernism, postmaterialism, and globalization.

KEY TERMS AND DEFINITIONS

1. _____ : condition arising when the legitimacy of traditional norms is challenged or these norms become ill-defined.

2. _____ : Tönnies' term, meaning society or association, for the cold, impersonal, and self-interested social relations of industrial cities.

3. _____ : control or exploitation of a country by another, often by conquest.

4. _____ : the theory that argues that the limited development of the Third World is a consequence of Third World factors such as traditional cultures, capital shortages, lack of technological expertise, etc.

5. _____ : integration based upon similarity.

6. _____ : Tönnies' term meaning community, describing the warm and intimate social relations he saw as occurring in agrarian communities prior to industrialization.

7. _____ : eighteenth-century movement championing free speech, freedom of conscience, equal rights, empiricism, skepticism, and reason.

8. _____ : integration based on cooperation of different parts.

9. _____ : the approach that divides countries into core, periphery, and semi-periphery and sees them as forming a unified system.

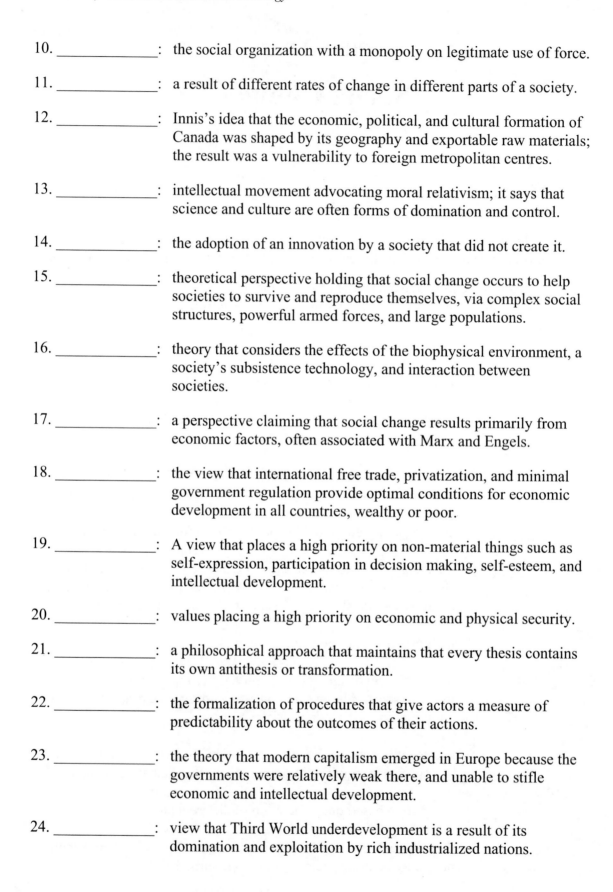

10. _____: the social organization with a monopoly on legitimate use of force.

11. _____: a result of different rates of change in different parts of a society.

12. _____: Innis's idea that the economic, political, and cultural formation of Canada was shaped by its geography and exportable raw materials; the result was a vulnerability to foreign metropolitan centres.

13. _____: intellectual movement advocating moral relativism; it says that science and culture are often forms of domination and control.

14. _____: the adoption of an innovation by a society that did not create it.

15. _____: theoretical perspective holding that social change occurs to help societies to survive and reproduce themselves, via complex social structures, powerful armed forces, and large populations.

16. _____: theory that considers the effects of the biophysical environment, a society's subsistence technology, and interaction between societies.

17. _____: a perspective claiming that social change results primarily from economic factors, often associated with Marx and Engels.

18. _____: the view that international free trade, privatization, and minimal government regulation provide optimal conditions for economic development in all countries, wealthy or poor.

19. _____: A view that places a high priority on non-material things such as self-expression, participation in decision making, self-esteem, and intellectual development.

20. _____: values placing a high priority on economic and physical security.

21. _____: a philosophical approach that maintains that every thesis contains its own antithesis or transformation.

22. _____: the formalization of procedures that give actors a measure of predictability about the outcomes of their actions.

23. _____: the theory that modern capitalism emerged in Europe because the governments were relatively weak there, and unable to stifle economic and intellectual development.

24. _____: view that Third World underdevelopment is a result of its domination and exploitation by rich industrialized nations.

SELF-QUIZ

1. Although there was great diversity among gathering and hunting societies, they were generally all of the following, except

   a) spiritual
   b) lacking a division of labour
   c) nomadic
   d) small
   e) sharing

2. Exploitation and pronounced inequality had their origin in _____ societies.

   a) farming
   b) industrial
   c) postindustrial
   d) hunting and gathering
   e) gathering and hunting

3. In farming societies, women generally had _____ power than men.
   a) more
   b) the same amount
   c) it depended; economically women had power, over defence, they did not
   d) less
   e) more institutionalized

4. The Enlightenment was not marked by

   a) skepticism
   b) reason
   c) observation
   d) pro-monarchy sentiment
   e) challenges to tradition

5. Spencer coined the phrase(s)

   a) survival of the fittest
   b) work is for life
   c) neo-evolutionism
   d) gathering and hunting
   e) a and b

6. Which order is chronologically correct?

   a) hunting/gathering, horticultural, postmodern, industrial
   b) horticultural, hunting/gathering, industrial, postmodern
   c) hunting/gathering, horticultural, industrial, postmodern
   d) hunting/gathering, horticultural, postmodern, industrial
   e) none of the above

7.   Anomie is more likely to be found in which type of society?

   a)   mechanical
   b)   organic
   c)   *gesellschaft*
   d)   *gemeinschaft*
   e)   b and c

8.   The _____ approach emphasizes change, conflict, and eventually demise.

   a)   positive
   b)   dialectical
   c)   evolutionary
   d)   neo-evolutionary
   e)   materialist

9.   The religion that Weber saw as the basis for capitalism is

   a)   Methodism
   b)   Islam
   c)   Roman Catholicism
   d)   Calvinism
   e)   Judaism

10.   A discussion of prior economies such as the one involving lords and serfs is part of whose theory of social change?

   a)   Comte
   b)   Spencer
   c)   Weber
   d)   Marx and Engels
   e)   a and b

11.   The "Great Disruption" does not encompass increasing

   a)   crime
   b)   divorce
   c)   religiosity
   d)   number of births out of wedlock
   e)   individualism

12.   That there are no facts, only interpretations, is a tenet of

   a)   postmaterialism
   b)   evolutionism
   c)   postmodernism
   d)   anomie
   e)   positivism

FILL IN THE BLANKS

1.   Social change, perhaps more than any other area of sociology, requires a
      _____ or international focus for its study.

2.   One major difference between earlier foraging societies and industrial societies is
      the existence of the formal _____, that body that can legitimately use
      force.

3.   Because hunting and gathering societies had virtually no _____, there
      was little opportunity for inequality and exploitation.

4.   Spencer is a founder of _____ theory.

5.   For Spencer, the growing differentiation and integration of society result
      primarily from _____.

6.   _____ technology is that needed to acquire the basic necessities of life;
      as it becomes more sophisticated, a society can evolve.

7.   The invention that lowered the status of women in farming is the _____.

8.   Innis's term for Canada's exportable fish, furs, lumber, and minerals:
      _____.

9.   For Comte, the three eras of social development were the theological, the
      metaphysical, and finally the scientific or _____ stage.

10.   It is here in which mainstream women imitate strippers and porn stars:
      _____.

11.   Historical materialism emphasizes material or _____ factors in
      explaining social change.

12.   Weber disagreed with Marx, and suggested that non-economic factors also can
      explain social change; Weber emphasized _____ factors, and more
      specifically _____.

Answers

KEY TERMS AND DEFINITIONS

1. anomie
2. *gesellschaft*
3. imperialism
4. modernization theory
5. mechanical solidarity
6. *gemeinschaft*
7. Enlightenment
8. organic solidarity
9. world system theory
10. state
11. cultural lag
12. staples thesis
13. postmodernism
14. diffusion
15. evolutionism
16. ecological-evolutionary theory
17. historical materialism
18. neo-liberalism
19. postmaterialism
20. materialist values
21. dialectical
22. rationalization
23. state theory of modernization
24. dependency theory

SELF-QUIZ

1. b
2. a
3. d
4. d
5. e
6. c
7. e
8. b
9. d
10. d
11. c
12. c

FILL IN THE BLANKS

1. comparative
2. state
3. surplus production
4. evolutionary
5. conflict
6. Subsistence
7. plough
8. staples
9. positive
10. "raunch" culture
11. economic
12. cultural, religion